ARE YOU SMARTER THAN A 5TH GRADER?

ARE YOU SMARTER THAN A 5TH GRADER?

**The Play-at-Home Companion
Book to the Hit TV Show!**

INTRODUCTION BY JEFF FOXWORTHY

MICHAEL BENSON

HARPER**ENTERTAINMENT**

NEW YORK · LONDON · TORONTO · SYDNEY

HARPER**ENTERTAINMENT**

FIRST EDITION

Designed by Laura Kaeppel

Library of Congress Cataloging-in-Publication Data is available upon request.

ISBN: 978-0-06-147306-7
ISBN-10: 0-06-147306-5

07 08 09 10 11   OV/RRD   10 9 8 7

To my favorite 5th Grader,
Matthew T. Benson

Acknowledgments

The author would like to express his deepest thanks to the masterful educators who have helped come up with the quiz questions for this book: Lori Piccininno, Lisa Amendolia, and Jim and Jackie Raleigh. Others, without whom the book couldn't have been written, include Bridget Agosta, Tekla Benson, Brian Chen, the Kids Hall of Fame, and Amazing-kids.org.

ARE YOU SMARTER THAN A 5TH GRADER?

Introduction

You know, when I got the call to be the host of *Are You Smarter Than A 5th Grader?* I thought somebody must have made a mistake. I mean, me, hosting a quiz show? I never thought I'd host a quiz show—I'm an idiot!

But then when I learned what the concept of the show was, I loved it. I thought, "I can do this. This is fun." There's no script—I don't know what the questions are going to be before they come up. I don't know what I'm going to say to the contestants. I'm just improvising my way through it. And my instinct was right. The show is a hit because it goes across so many lines. Kids and their parents can watch it together. You can get the grandparents in there too. And your cousins. And the dog. It really works for everyone ages five to ninety.

Kids like the show because it shows them beating adults at something, and I don't mean like when you let your kid beat you at checkers. Adults like it because a) it's something they can watch with their kids, and b) every adult secretly thinks they can do it. And then they start the game and they realize pretty quickly . . . they can't. Adults think "I'm an accountant," or "I'm a lawyer." But they haven't seen these questions in twenty or thirty years. Hey, I'm glad I'm not standing there having to answer 'em for money. It'd be sad . . . there'd be a lot of peanut butter and jelly sandwiches around my house. I'd say I know the right answer about 40 to 50 percent of the time. The other times, I'm like a dog looking at a ceiling fan—I have no idea.

I get along great with the kids—even though they're a lot smarter than I am. I just let them be kids. During the breaks one of 'em will say, "Jeff, look, I brought my pogo stick in today!" And then I'll try out the pogo stick, trying not to break my neck. They get a big kick out of that.

Now when I was in the 5th grade, I went to Mitchell Road Elementary School in Greenville, South Carolina. I was about fourteen at the time. Actually, I did pretty good—A's and B's. But I remember getting those notes from the teacher on the comment part of the report card—"Jeff talks too much in class. What does he think he is—a comedian?" Well, things seem to have come full circle. I was trying to make the class laugh in 5th grade and was getting in trouble for it . . . now, I'm still trying to make the 5th grade class laugh but I'm getting paid for it!

What's great about the book version of *Are You Smarter Than A 5th Grader?* is that you don't have to be in front of a TV to play along with the game. You or your kids or your friends can take it with you wherever you go—in a car, truck, plane, or maybe even just sitting in your living room. Works in the bathroom, too, but not in the shower, if you know what I mean. You've got seventy-five tests you can take with no pressure at all—no TV cameras, no money on the line, and no F to go on your permanent record. The book even includes some of the questions we used on the air—so you can see if you really *are* smarter than a 5th grader. But make sure you have a mirror handy just in case you're not. Be honest with yourself! I won't hold it against you.

Jeff Foxworthy

1ST GRADE ▪ SOCIAL STUDIES

In what month do Americans go trick-or-treating?

1ST GRADE ▪ WORLD GEOGRAPHY

❏ **True**   ❏ **False**

Africa is a country south of Europe.

2ND GRADE ▪ U.S. GEOGRAPHY

What is the body of water between Florida and Texas called?

2ND GRADE ▪ ENGLISH

How many syllables are there in the word Mississippi?

3RD GRADE ▪ WORLD HISTORY

❏ **True**   ❏ **False**

Columbus discovered America in the fourteenth century.

3RD GRADE ▪ MEASUREMENTS

How many feet are there in 75 yards?

4TH GRADE ▪ EARTH SCIENCE

❏ True   ❏ False

Comets are made up mostly of rock and metal.

4TH GRADE ▪ CHEMISTRY

On the periodic table, what element is represented by the letter N?

5TH GRADE ▪ MATH

Is the fraction $3/7$ greater than or less than $7/10$?

5TH GRADE ▪ BIOLOGY

The frontal lobe of your brain controls . . .

○ A. your learning and decision making

○ B. your hearing and memory

○ C. your sense of touch

○ D. your sight

$1,000,000 Question

5TH GRADE ▪ MUSIC

In classical music, what instruments typically comprise a string quartet?

5th Grade Fun Fact . . . When he was old enough to be a fifth grader, composer Wolfgang Amadeus Mozart was already writing symphonies!

1ST GRADE ▪ U.S. HISTORY

Who was President of the United States before George W. Bush?

1ST GRADE ▪ ENGLISH

Which is the verb in the following sentence?
"She ran all the way home."

2ND GRADE ▪ MEASUREMENTS

How many inches are there in two yards?

2ND GRADE ▪ GOVERNMENT

What is the capital of New York State?

3RD GRADE ▪ EARTH SCIENCE

What is the longest river in the United States?
- ○ A. The Missouri
- ○ B. The Mississippi
- ○ C. The Rio Grande
- ○ D. The Ohio

3RD GRADE ▪ HUMAN SCIENCE

What is the clinical name for the thigh bone?

4TH GRADE ▪ MATH

If a backyard is 50 feet long and 20 feet wide, how many square feet is the yard?

4TH GRADE • CHEMISTRY

Which is not true about carbon dioxide (CO_2)?

- ○ A. It's called dry ice in its solid form.
- ○ B. It contributes to global warming.
- ○ C. It is colorless, odorless and tasteless.
- ○ D. It is a noble gas.

5TH GRADE • U.S. HISTORY

Who did not sign the U.S. Constitution?

- ○ A. George Washington
- ○ B. John Hancock
- ○ C. Ben Franklin
- ○ D. Alexander Hamilton

5TH GRADE • CHEMISTRY

Common table salt is a chemical compound of . . .

- ○ A. Sodium and chlorine
- ○ B. Sodium and chromium
- ○ C. Magnesium and potassium
- ○ D. Sodium and magnesium

$1,000,000 Question

5TH GRADE • ANIMAL SCIENCE

What lizard has three eyes?

5th Grade Superstar . . . By the time Shirley Temple was in fifth grade she had already starred in 25 movies!

1st Grade ▪ Art

What color comes from mixing equal parts red with white paint?

1st Grade ▪ Science

What are the three states of matter?

2nd Grade ▪ English

In the word "unnecessary," what is the prefix?

2nd Grade ▪ Grammar

What is the plural form for the word "deer"?

3rd Grade ▪ Geography

What is the largest ocean on Earth?

3rd Grade ▪ U.S. History

What event was part of the reason the United States entered World War II?

○ A. The sinking of the *Lusitania*

○ B. The sinking of the *Maine*

○ C. The sinking of the *Arizona*

○ D. The capture of the *Pueblo*

4TH GRADE ▪ MATH

Between 1 and 100, how many multiples of 7 are odd numbers?

4TH GRADE ▪ HUMAN SCIENCE

Which of the following human glands is found in the brain?

○ A. Prostate   ○ C. Thyroid

○ B. Pituitary   ○ D. Lymph

5TH GRADE ▪ MATH

What is the lowest common denominator for $3/4$ and $4/7$?

5TH GRADE ▪ U.S. HISTORY

Who was the first American in space?

$1,000,000 Question

5TH GRADE ▪ GEOMETRY

What is an octahedron?

> **Special Teachers ... Los Angeles 5th grade teacher Rafe Esquith was honored on television for working 12-hour days so he could teach students advanced math, music, and Shakespeare both before and after school. Mr. Esquith teaches at Hobart Boulevard Elementary School in L.A.**

1ST GRADE ▪ SCIENCE

What gas do humans need to breathe in order to live?

1ST GRADE ▪ U.S. GEOGRAPHY

Maine borders which U.S. state?

2ND GRADE ▪ MATH

How much is 14 times 5?

○ A. 65   ○ C. 75

○ B. 50   ○ D. 70

2ND GRADE ▪ WORLD GEOGRAPHY

What country has the longest border with the United States?

3RD GRADE ▪ MUSIC

Which of the following is a percussion instrument?

○ A. Piano   ○ C. Guitar

○ B. Clarinet   ○ D. Drums

3RD GRADE ▪ U.S. HISTORY

Which Civil War battle took place the farthest north?

In colonial America, what was the Sugar Act?

○ A. A law prohibiting the growing of sugar

○ B. A tax on molasses and wine

○ C. A law regulating the amount of sugar in candy

○ D. A musical comedy act by the Sugar Sisters from London

4TH GRADE • MATH

Trina, Tim, and Mark have 2,142 baseball cards. If they divide the cards evenly, how many will each child have?

5TH GRADE • ART

Who painted the *Mona Lisa*?

○ A. Michelangelo   ○ C. da Vinci

○ B. Rembrandt   ○ D. van Gogh

5TH GRADE • GEOGRAPHY

❑ **True**   ❑ **False**

Ohio shares a border with Illinois.

$1,000,000 Question

5TH GRADE • U.S. HISTORY

Which general led U.S. troops during the Vietnam War?

1ST GRADE ▪ SCIENCE

❑ **True**   ❑ **False**

The biggest fish is a whale.

1ST GRADE ▪ HISTORY

Who invented the lightbulb?

2ND GRADE ▪ MATH

How many times does 7 divide into 49?

○ A. 6   ○ C. 7

○ B. 5   ○ D. 8

2ND GRADE ▪ SPELLING

Witch word is misspelled?

3RD GRADE ▪ SCIENCE

What does a paleontologist study?

3RD GRADE ▪ GEOGRAPHY

The Tropic of Capricorn lies in which hemisphere?

4TH GRADE ▪ PUNCTUATION

Which sentence is incorrect?

○ A. Absence makes the heart grow fonder.

○ B. The dog won't eat it's food.

○ C. There's their mother over there.

○ D. The Yankees is a great team.

4TH GRADE ▪ U.S. HISTORY

The Mason-Dixon Line was created . . .

○ A. As a route for westward expansion

○ B. To solve a property dispute

○ C. To divide Free states from Slave states

○ D. To transmit the first phone call

5TH GRADE ▪ ASTRONOMY

What are the large rocks that orbit the sun between Mars and Jupiter called?

5TH GRADE ▪ SCIENCE

Which of the following is necessary for photosynthesis?

○ A. Wind

○ B. Quiet

○ C. Low atmospheric pressure

○ D. Sunshine

$1,000,000 Question

5TH GRADE ▪ BIOLOGY

What is the smallest fish in the world?

QUIZ NUMBER 6

First Grade ▪ Measurements

How many inches are in a foot?

First Grade ▪ Social Studies

Whose picture is on the five-dollar bill?

2nd Grade ▪ Astronomy

Which planet in our solar system is known for its beautiful rings?

2nd Grade ▪ Math

How many zeroes are in the numeral for one million?

3rd Grade ▪ Geography

What is the longest river in the world?

- ○ A. Yangtze
- ○ B. Nile
- ○ C. Amazon
- ○ D. Mississippi

3rd Grade ▪ Math

Complete this problem: $3/4 + 1/2 =$

- ○ A. $3/8$
- ○ B. $4/8$
- ○ C. $6/4$
- ○ D. $5/4$

4TH GRADE • EARTH SCIENCE

Which is the hardest mineral?

4TH GRADE • U.S. HISTORY

During World War II, on the day known as D-Day, at what location did allied troops invade Europe?

5TH GRADE • MATH

What whole number is closest to the square root of 65?

5TH GRADE • SCIENCE

If a student wanted to measure the absorbency of different types of soil, she would put an identical amount of each type of soil into identical pots, each with a hole in the bottom. She would then pour the same amount of water into each pot and measure . . .

- ○ A. how fast plants grew in each pot.
- ○ B. how long it takes water to come out of the hole at the bottom.
- ○ C. the amount of water that comes out of the hole in the bottom.
- ○ D. the relative acidity of the soil after the water is added.

$1,000,000 Question

5TH GRADE • MATH

How is 131 centimeters expressed in meters?

1st Grade • English

How many adjectives are in the sentence: "Billy made a rude noise in class."

1st Grade • Animal Science

❑ **True**   ❑ **False**

A lizard is a reptile.

2nd Grade • Animal Science

❑ **True**   ❑ **False**

The kangaroo is a marsupial.

2nd Grade • World History

The ancient Egyptian empire was based on what continent?

3rd Grade • Geometry

How many sides does a quadrangle have?

3rd Grade • World Geography

What land mass on Earth is known as the "Island Continent"?

4TH GRADE ▪ U.S. HISTORY

❏ True ❏ False

George H. W. Bush and George W. Bush are the only father and son to both become presidents of the United States.

4TH GRADE ▪ WORLD GEOGRAPHY

What is the easternmost country in Africa?

○ A. Gabon ○ C. Eritrea

○ B. Somalia ○ D. Sudan

5TH GRADE ▪ SCIENCE

The outermost part of an animal cell is known as the . . .

○ A. Ribosome ○ C. Nucleolus

○ B. Nucleus ○ D. Membrane

5TH GRADE ▪ HISTORY

Which was invented first?

○ A. Telegraph ○ C. Neon lamp

○ B. Motorized vacuum cleaner ○ D. Airplane

$1,000,000 Question

5TH GRADE ▪ SPELLING

What state is Boston in? Spelling counts!

The Results Are In! According to the American School Counselor Association, the average fifth grader has a positive approach to life.

1st Grade ▪ Math

How many seconds are in a minute?

1st Grade ▪ English

Which is the noun in the sentence?
"The chair is rocking slowly."

2nd Grade ▪ Spelling

Which U.S. state comes first alphabetically?

2nd Grade ▪ Animal Science

The kangaroo's natural habitat is on what continent?

3rd Grade ▪ Math

How many times do parallel lines intersect?

3rd Grade ▪ Earth Science

What type of rock comes out of a volcano?

○ A. Metamorphic   ○ C. Igneous

○ B. Sedimentary   ○ D. Granite

4th Grade ▪ Measurements

How many ounces are in a quart?

Which waterway connects the Atlantic and Pacific Oceans?

○ A. Suez Canal   ○ C. Panama Canal

○ B. Erie Canal   ○ D. Columbia River

5TH GRADE • MATH

What is the remainder when you divide the square root of 16 into 17?

5TH GRADE • SCIENCE

Which is not a product of photosynthesis: sugar, oxygen, or carbon dioxide?

$1,000,000 Question

5TH GRADE • MUSIC

How many quarter notes are in a measure played in a 4/4 time signature?

> **Didja Know . . . Gregory R. Smith, born in 1989, entered college at age 10 and was first nominated for the Nobel Peace Prize at age 12. Today he is a children's rights advocate who speaks at conferences for a wide variety of humanitarian causes.**

1ST GRADE ▪ GRAMMAR

How many proper nouns are there in the following sentence? "I heard that Bill bought a house in Oklahoma."

1ST GRADE ▪ MEASUREMENTS

How many months in the year have only thirty days?

2ND GRADE ▪ U.S. HISTORY

What is the name of the mountain that has the likenesses of four presidents carved into it?

2ND GRADE ▪ U.S. GEOGRAPHY

Which city has the second-largest population?

○ A. Chicago   ○ C. New York City

○ B. Houston   ○ D. Los Angeles

3RD GRADE ▪ MATH

What is the correct way to say the number "four point zero seven"?

3RD GRADE ▪ SCIENCE

What is the uppermost layer of Earth's atmosphere called?

4TH GRADE ▪ U.S. HISTORY

What three countries comprised the axis powers during World War II?

4TH GRADE ▪ MUSIC

In an orchestra, the trombones are in the _____ section.

- ○ A. percussion
- ○ B. brass
- ○ C. woodwind
- ○ D. string

5TH GRADE ▪ SOCIAL STUDIES

The Blackfoot Indians of the northern plain states got their name by . . .

- ○ A. walking across tar.
- ○ B. having naturally dark feet.
- ○ C. dying their shoes black.
- ○ D. running without leaving footprints.

5TH GRADE ▪ ENGLISH

In which play did Shakespeare write, "To be or not to be, that is the question."

$1,000,000 Question

5TH GRADE ▪ GEOMETRY

How many degrees are in a straight angle?

1ST GRADE ▪ ENGLISH

How many consonants are in the word "baseball"?

1ST GRADE ▪ MEASUREMENTS

How many days are there in a non-leap year?

2ND GRADE ▪ MATH

How many nickels are there in two dollars?

2ND GRADE ▪ SPELLING

Spell the word that means "full of beauty."

3RD GRADE ▪ MATH

❏ **True**   ❏ **False**

$3/5 - 2/5 = (3 - 2)/5$

3RD GRADE ▪ SCIENCE

❏ **True**   ❏ **False**

A chameleon cannot turn pink.

4TH GRADE ▪ SCIENCE

What is a light-year?

4TH GRADE ▪ EARTH SCIENCE

When you are in New Zealand, in what month is the winter solstice?

5TH GRADE ▪ WORLD HISTORY

John Cabot, Henry Hudson, and Ferdinand Magellan were all . . .

- ○ A. rulers.
- ○ B. scientists.
- ○ C. inventors.
- ○ D. explorers.

5TH GRADE ▪ U.S. GEOGRAPHY

What four U.S. states form the "Four Corners" in the American southwest?

$1,000,000 Question

5TH GRADE ▪ SCIENCE

An average room full of air weighs closest to which amount?

- ○ A. 10 pounds
- ○ B. 100 pounds
- ○ C. 1 pound
- ○ D. 1 ounce

**I'd-Like-To-Thank-The-Little-People Award . . .
Tatum O'Neal won the Best Supporting
Actress Oscar at age 10 for her 1973 role in
Paper Moon, making her the youngest person
ever to win a regularly awarded Oscar.**

1ST GRADE ▪ MATH

If you find a penny on the ground once a day for two weeks, how many cents do you have?

1ST GRADE ▪ SCIENCE

❏ **True**   ❏ **False**

Mammals are warm-blooded creatures.

2ND GRADE ▪ SOCIAL STUDIES

❏ **True**   ❏ **False**

All Hispanics are from Mexico.

2ND GRADE ▪ GRAMMAR

What is the preferred plural of the word "octopus"?

○ A. Octopusses   ○ C. Octopi

○ B. Octopods   ○ D. Octoroons

3RD GRADE ▪ MATH

The answer to a subtraction problem is called the

_____.

3RD GRADE ▪ HEALTH

Which is a consumer in a food chain?

- ○ A. Corn
- ○ B. A chicken
- ○ C. Hay
- ○ D. Carrots

4TH GRADE ▪ ASTRONOMY

The Big Dipper is part of the constellation Ursa Major. What does "ursa major" mean in English?

4TH GRADE ▪ CHEMISTRY

On the periodic table, what element is represented by the letter C?

5TH GRADE ▪ HISTORY

In which year did John Rolfe marry Pocahontas?

- ○ A. 1514
- ○ B. 1614
- ○ C. 1714
- ○ D. 1814

5TH GRADE ▪ EARTH SCIENCE

The type of waves created by an earthquake are called _____.

- ○ A. Plasmatic
- ○ B. Ecstatic
- ○ C. Seismic
- ○ D. Volcanic

$1,000,000 Question

5TH GRADE ▪ MUSIC

In classical music, the "Ode to Joy" comes in which of Beethoven's symphonies?

1st Grade ▪ Math

If it is 2:43 P.M., in how many minutes will it be until the school bell rings at 3:00 P.M.?

1st Grade ▪ Music

How many strings does a typical guitar have?

2nd Grade ▪ English

What is the adjective in this sentence?
"I love the blue sky."

2nd Grade ▪ Phys. Ed.

Which is not true of the exercise known as jumping jacks?

- ○ A. They are done standing up.
- ○ B. You clap your hands above your head.
- ○ C. You move both your feet at the same time.
- ○ D. You turn your head from side to side.

3rd Grade ▪ English

How many adverbs are in the sentence?
"Our portly dad loudly belches."

3RD GRADE ▪ HUMAN SCIENCE

❑ **True**   ❑ **False**

The smallest bone in the human body is in the foot.

4TH GRADE ▪ PHYSICS

A moving object tends to continue moving unless something stops it. That's the Law of:

○ A. Gravity.   ○ C. Inertia.

○ B. Revolution.   ○ D. the Land.

4TH GRADE ▪ U.S. HISTORY

Who was U.S. president during most of World War II?

5TH GRADE ▪ SCIENCE

What does the acronym "sonar" stand for?

5TH GRADE ▪ ANCIENT HISTORY

In which century did Alexander the Great live?

○ A. 2nd century A.D.   ○ C. 1st century A.D.

○ B. 4th century B.C.   ○ D. 5th century B.C.

$1,000,000 Question

5TH GRADE ▪ SPELLING

Spell the name of Native American shoes made from animal hide.

1ST GRADE ▪ ENGLISH

In Mother Goose, who is under a haystack fast asleep?

1ST GRADE ▪ MATH

If a touchdown is worth six points, and an extra point is worth one, how many touchdowns and extra points would a team have to score to have 35 points?

2ND GRADE ▪ ENGLISH

In the word "directly," what is the suffix?

2ND GRADE ▪ DANCE

What type of dancers dance on their toes?

3RD GRADE ▪ U.S. HISTORY

Who was the first American to orbit the Earth in space?

3RD GRADE ▪ BIOLOGY

Which side of the human heart pumps the blood out to most of the body?

○ A. Left   ○ C. Top

○ B. Right   ○ D. Bottom

4TH GRADE ▪ GEOGRAPHY

What is the name of the mountain range in Switzerland?

4TH GRADE ▪ U.S. HISTORY

In 1869, the first transcontinental railroad was completed in what state?

○ A. California   ○ C. Colorado

○ B. Utah   ○ D. Idaho

5TH GRADE ▪ HISTORY

In what year did English settlers first land at Jamestown, Virginia?

○ A. 1492   ○ C. 1707

○ B. 1607   ○ D. 1621

5TH GRADE ▪ LITERATURE

Who wrote *The Wizard of Oz*?

$1,000,000 Question

5TH GRADE ▪ WORLD GEOGRAPHY

Andorra lies between what two European countries?

> **This-Doesn't-Need-No-Stinkin'-Pencil Award Goes to . . . Zerah Colburn, who by age 10, was able to multiply six-digit numbers in his head.**

1ST GRADE ▪ MEASUREMENTS

How many years are in a century?

1ST GRADE ▪ U.S. GEOGRAPHY

With which three U.S. states does California share a border?

2ND GRADE ▪ ANIMAL SCIENCE

Which type of bird lays the largest eggs?

2ND GRADE ▪ MUSIC

Which is not a job of the orchestra's conductor?

○ A. Determines how fast the music is played

○ B. Keeps the musicians playing together

○ C. Writes the music

○ D. Leads rehearsals

3RD GRADE ▪ ART

Who painted the ceiling of the Sistine Chapel?

3RD GRADE ▪ MATH

Is 9 × 39 less, equal, or more than 360?

Antibiotics kill _____.

○ A. Viruses   ○ C. Odors

○ B. Chlorophyll   ○ D. Bacteria

4TH GRADE ▪ MATH

If a field is 30 yards wide and 150 yards long, how many square yards is the field?

5TH GRADE ▪ U.S. GEOGRAPHY

Hoover Dam is on the border between what two U.S. states?

5TH GRADE ▪ U.S. HISTORY

To what political party did Abraham Lincoln belong?

$1,000,000 Question

5TH GRADE ▪ SCIENCE

What is dendochronology?

○ A. Determining the age of ancient objects

○ B. Counting the rings in a tree stump to determine the age of the tree

○ C. Telling time using the sun

○ D. Making sure events are remembered in the order they happened

1ST GRADE • ART

Which of the following is *not* a primary color?

○ A. Red   ○ C. Yellow

○ B. Blue   ○ D. Green

1ST GRADE • ANIMAL SCIENCE

❏ **True**   ❏ **False**

Turtles are cold-blooded.

2ND GRADE • WORLD GEOGRAPHY

Canada is on which continent?

2ND GRADE • GRAMMAR

How many singular nouns are there in the following sentence? "Billy went to the ballpark to see the Rangers play the Angels."

3RD GRADE • SPELLING

Spell the name of the holiday in September that honors the American work force.

3RD GRADE • MATH

If $6 + n = 15$, what is n?

4TH GRADE ▪ MUSIC

In what country was the classical-music composer Johann Sebastian Bach born?

- ○ A. Germany
- ○ B. Belgium
- ○ C. France
- ○ D. Switzerland

4TH GRADE ▪ GEOGRAPHY

What is the tallest mountain in Africa?

5TH GRADE ▪ ASTRONOMY

"Shooting stars" are not really stars at all. They are _____.

5TH GRADE ▪ U.S. HISTORY

Who was the first U.S. president to be born in a hospital?

- ○ A. Nixon
- ○ B. Taft
- ○ C. Carter
- ○ D. Kennedy

$1,000,000 Question

5TH GRADE ▪ ANIMAL SCIENCE

What is the world's longest insect?

The Results Are In! According to the American School Counselor Association, the average 5th grader tends to be obedient, good-natured and fun.

1ST GRADE • ENGLISH

What is the subject of the following sentence?
"My mother is always good to me."

1ST GRADE • SOCIAL STUDIES

In American coins, whose likeness is on the nickel?

2ND GRADE • MATH

$3 \times 133 =$ _____

2ND GRADE • MEASUREMENTS

How many centimeters are in a meter?

3RD GRADE • BIOLOGY

❑ **True**   ❑ **False**

Humans have a large, medium, and small intestine.

3RD GRADE • MAPS

Which of the following does a relief map show?

○ A. Topography   ○ C. Temperature

○ B. Population   ○ D. Political affiliation

4TH GRADE ▪ ANIMAL SCIENCE

On which continent are you unlikely to find a badger?

○ A. North America   ○ C. Europe

○ B. Africa   ○ D. Asia

4TH GRADE ▪ WORLD GEOGRAPHY

The Bahamas are part of which chain of islands?

○ A. Marianas   ○ C. West Indies

○ B. Canaries   ○ D. Aleutians

5TH GRADE ▪ WORLD HISTORY

Who was the first European explorer to cross the New World east to west and gaze upon the Pacific?

○ A. De Soto   ○ C. Balboa

○ B. Cortez   ○ D. Magellan

5TH GRADE ▪ U.S. HISTORY

In 1850, from which country did most U.S. immigrants come?

○ A. Germany   ○ C. Mexico

○ B. Ireland   ○ D. China

$1,000,000 Question

5TH GRADE ▪ MATH

What are the prime numbers between 0 and 10?

1ST GRADE ▪ MUSIC

Which of the following musical instruments is not a woodwind?

- ○ A. English Horn
- ○ B. Flute
- ○ C. Bass clarinet
- ○ D. Tuba

1ST GRADE ▪ SPELLING

Spelling the missing word: "There are no essays on the test. It's all multiple _____."

2ND GRADE ▪ ENGLISH

What is the adverb in the following sentence? "The fox ran quickly through the woods."

2ND GRADE ▪ MEASUREMENTS

Using U.S. coins, what are the fewest number of coins you need to make exactly 63 cents?

3RD GRADE ▪ MATH

How many sides does a pentagon have?

3RD GRADE ▪ BIOLOGY

In the human body, which system is the liver in?

- ○ A. Respiratory
- ○ B. Digestive
- ○ C. Circulatory
- ○ D. Nervous

4TH GRADE ▪ GEOGRAPHY

What is the westernmost country in Africa?

- ○ A. Liberia
- ○ B. Uganda
- ○ C. Senegal
- ○ D. Djibouti

4TH GRADE ▪ PHYS. ED.

In professional baseball, the pitching rubber is 60 feet 6 inches from home plate. What is the distance in Little League baseball?

5TH GRADE ▪ HEALTH

Which is an example of a legume?

- ○ A. Carrot
- ○ B. Radish
- ○ C. Bean
- ○ D. Spaghetti

5TH GRADE ▪ BIOLOGY

In which part of a cell is the DNA found?

$1,000,000 Question

5TH GRADE ▪ HISTORY

Which of these was invented first?

- ○ A. Windshield wipers
- ○ B. Cornflakes
- ○ C. Color photography
- ○ D. Cellophane

1ST GRADE ▪ MEASUREMENTS

If you laid three yardsticks and a 12-inch ruler end to end, how long would it be in feet?

1ST GRADE ▪ ANIMAL SCIENCE

A human being is a(n) _____.

- ○ A. Marsupial
- ○ B. Amphibian
- ○ C. Mammal
- ○ D. Reptile

2ND GRADE ▪ ENGLISH

In the word "stone," which letter is silent?

2ND GRADE ▪ ANIMAL SCIENCE

The easiest way to tell the difference between an African and an Asian elephant is by the size of its . . .

- ○ A. Tusks
- ○ B. Feet
- ○ C. Eyes
- ○ D. Ears

3RD GRADE ▪ MATH

❏ **True**   ❏ **False**

The base is the longest side of an equilateral triangle.

3RD GRADE ▪ U.S. HISTORY

What U.S. state was formed as a result of the Civil War?

4TH GRADE ▪ WORLD GEOGRAPHY

On what continent is Bolivia?

○ A. North America   ○ C. South America

○ B. Europe   ○ D. Africa

4TH GRADE ▪ SCIENCE

What does a botanist study?

5TH GRADE ▪ EARTH SCIENCE

The process of rocks breaking down is called _____.

○ A. Evolution   ○ C. Weathering

○ B. Liberation   ○ D. Metamorphosis

5TH GRADE ▪ PHYS. ED.

Who wrote the first set of rules for boxing?

○ A. King Henry VIII

○ B. John L. Sullivan

○ C. The Marquess of Queensbury

○ D. The Duke of Edinburgh

$1,000,000 Question

5TH GRADE ▪ U.S. HISTORY

During which decade were there women known as "flappers?"

QUIZ NUMBER 19

1ST GRADE • GRAMMAR

How many proper nouns are in the following sentence? "In Pennsylvania, Petula met my dog, Popcorn."

1ST GRADE • SOCIAL STUDIES

What alphabet of raised dots allows blind people to read?

2ND GRADE • SPELLING

Which U.S. state comes last alphabetically?

2ND GRADE • HISTORY

❑ **True**   ❑ **False**

The 17th century is also known as the 1800s.

3RD GRADE • SCIENCE

In what layer of Earth's atmosphere do jet aircraft usually fly?

3RD GRADE • MATH

Five baseball teams have 26 players each. How many ballplayers are there all together?

In which war were most of the battles fought in Cuba?

○ A. Mexican War ○ C. Spanish-American War

○ B. War of 1812 ○ D. Falklands War

Which is not part of the human circulatory system?

○ A. Ligaments ○ C. Veins

○ B. Capillaries ○ D. Arteries

Who wrote *Uncle Tom's Cabin*?

There's a movie called *Pirates of the* _____.
Spell the missing word.

$1,000,000 Question

How long is a micron?

○ A. $1/10{,}000$ of a millimeter

○ B. $1/1{,}000$ of a meter

○ C. $1/1{,}000{,}000$ of a meter

○ D. $1/10$ of a centimeter

**The Heroes Next Door Project . . . The 5th graders
in Sharon, Massachusetts, recently learned about
heroes. But they didn't learn out of a book. Instead
they visited real live heroes in their community!**

WHAT STAR IS CLOSEST TO EARTH?

=9
=16
25
36
49

QUIZ NUMBER 20

1ST GRADE ▪ ENGLISH

A, E, I, O and U are known as what?

1ST GRADE ▪ HEALTH

Which food has no seeds?

○ A. Tomato   ○ C. Banana

○ B. Apple   ○ D. Carrot

2ND GRADE ▪ SCIENCE

Much of America was carved out by large sheets of moving ice called _____.

2ND GRADE ▪ ENGLISH

Alice, Ann and Aimee sit in alphabetical order. Who sits third?

3RD GRADE ▪ SOCIAL STUDIES

❏ **True**   ❏ **False**

U.S. states have their own constitutions.

3RD GRADE ▪ MATH

What are the least number of ninths you would need to have more than a half?

Which U.S. presidents have their likenesses carved into Mount Rushmore?

Who carved "The Statue of David"?

During the Civil War, who was the president of the Confederate States of America?

What do the letters FBI stand for?

$1,000,000 Question

Which of the following cannot be classified as a terrestrial biome?

- ○ A. Desert
- ○ B. Jungle
- ○ C. Forest
- ○ D. Ocean

Quizmaster . . . Jeff Foxworthy, the hilarious host of *Are You Smarter Than a 5th Grader?*, is the biggest-selling comedy-recording artist in history. A multiple Grammy Award nominee and the best-selling author of more than 20 books, Foxworthy has also starred in all three "Blue Collar Comedy" tour movies. The 2006 soundtrack to Foxworthy's "Blue Collar Comedy Tour: One for the Road" was nominated for a Grammy Award.

QUIZ NUMBER 21

1ST GRADE ▪ HISTORY

What famous device did Alexander Graham Bell invent?

1ST GRADE ▪ U.S. GEOGRAPHY

❑ **True**   ❑ **False**

Georgia borders on the Gulf of Mexico.

2ND GRADE ▪ MATH

The answer to a multiplication problem is called the

_____.

2ND GRADE ▪ DANCE

What type of dance features the *do-si-do*?

3RD GRADE ▪ VOCABULARY

When you dilute something, do you make it weaker
or stronger?

3RD GRADE ▪ U.S. HISTORY

In U.S. history, what is the name of the document
that freed the slaves?

○ A. The Dred Scott Decision

○ B. The Emancipation Proclamation

○ C. The Gettysburg Address

○ D. The Freedom Act of 1863

4TH GRADE ▪ ASTRONOMY

What is the nearest star to the Earth?

4TH GRADE ▪ CHEMISTRY

On the periodic table, what element is represented by the letter O?

5TH GRADE ▪ MATH

Which two integers have a difference of 1 and a sum of 59?

5TH GRADE ▪ WORLD GEOGRAPHY

On what continent is the nation of Benin?

$1,000,000 Question

5TH GRADE ▪ WORLD HISTORY

In what century was the bicycle invented?

**5th Graders Who Made a Difference . . .
Macallan Durkin wanted to help food
programs in North Africa, a cause she learned
about when she lived for 3 years in Botswana.
She made and sold items to raise money,
including T-shirts with her own ostrich drawing
and "Don't Bury Your Head in the Sand" logo.**

1ST GRADE ▪ PHYS. ED.

Which member of the soccer team often wears gloves while playing?

1ST GRADE ▪ U.S. HISTORY

What document was signed on July 4, 1776?

- ○ A. The Articles of Confederation
- ○ B. The Treaty of Ghent
- ○ C. The Manifest Destiny
- ○ D. The Declaration of Independence

2ND GRADE ▪ ENGLISH

What is the present tense of "forgot"?

2ND GRADE ▪ WORLD GEOGRAPHY

Peru is on which continent?

3RD GRADE ▪ SPELLING

Spell the opposite of horizontal.

3RD GRADE ▪ HUMAN SCIENCE

❑ **True**   ❑ **False**

The human knuckle is an example of a ball-and-socket joint.

4TH GRADE ▪ MATH

If the dance floor is fifteen feet wide and twenty feet long, how many square feet is the dance floor?

4TH GRADE ▪ SOCIAL STUDIES

The first Thanksgiving took place in which colony?

○ A. Virginia

○ C. Massachusetts

○ B. Pennsylvania

○ D. New Jersey

5TH GRADE ▪ PHYS. ED.

What sport was originally known as "sidewalk surfing"?

5TH GRADE ▪ BIOLOGY

Which cannot be found in an animal cell?

○ A. Granule

○ C. Chloroplast

○ B. Mitochondrion

○ D. Nucleus

$1,000,000 Question

5TH GRADE ▪ ENGLISH

Who wrote *Alice's Adventures in Wonderland*?

But Can He Cross the Street Alone?
By the time he was as old as the other
5th graders, Tathagat Avatar Tulsi
already had his bachelor's degree!

1st Grade · Math

How much is 8 + 7?

1st Grade · U.S. History

Who was the third president of the United States?

2nd Grade · Music

A type of music in which musicians often improvise is called _____.

○ A. Disco

○ C. Jazz

○ B. Chamber music

○ D. Baroque

2nd Grade · Animal Science

Where are you most apt to find a chimpanzee in its natural habitat?

○ A. North America

○ C. Asia

○ B. South America

○ D. Africa

3rd Grade · Grammar

What is the compound word in this sentence?
"Baseball is the favorite game of kids at my school."

3RD GRADE ▪ CHEMISTRY

Which has different types of atoms joined tightly together?

- ○ A. Solution
- ○ B. Compound
- ○ C. Mixture
- ○ D. Element

4TH GRADE ▪ GEOGRAPHY

What is the tallest mountain in Europe?

4TH GRADE ▪ U.S. HISTORY

Who was the second man to walk on the Moon?

5TH GRADE ▪ SCIENCE

What type of clouds accompany a thunder storm?

5TH GRADE ▪ ENGLISH

Which word means "exquisitely fine"?

- ○ A. Sensitive
- ○ B. Fragile
- ○ C. Filagreed
- ○ D. Delicate

$1,000,000 Question

5TH GRADE ▪ SPELLING

Spell the missing word: "Tom Sawyer and _____ Finn."

5th Grade Heroes . . . 10-year-old Tilly Smith saved hundreds of lives in 2004. She was on vacation at a beach in Thailand and recognized the early signs of a *tsunami*. She told her parents and the area was cleared of people before it was engulfed with water.

QUIZ NUMBER 24

1ST GRADE ▪ ENGLISH

In fairy tales, who stuck in his thumb and pulled out a plum?

1ST GRADE ▪ U.S. GEOGRAPHY

What U.S. states does Hawaii share a border with?

2ND GRADE ▪ MAPS

If you're reading a map upon which one inch equals 100 miles, how many inches will 600 miles be?

2ND GRADE ▪ SCIENCE

A piece of glass that separates sunlight into colors is called _____.

- ○ A. A prism
- ○ B. Stained glass
- ○ C. A convex lens
- ○ D. A concave lens

3RD GRADE ▪ MEASUREMENTS

Which is warmer: 0 degrees Celsius or 30 degrees Fahrenheit?

3RD GRADE ▪ SPELLING

Spell the name of the most famous Queen of Egypt.

4TH GRADE • U.S. GEOGRAPHY

What state in the United States is known as the "Cotton State"?

○ A. Mississippi ○ C. Alabama

○ B. Oregon ○ D. Colorado

4TH GRADE • U.S. HISTORY

Who is the only U.S. president to serve two non-consecutive terms of office?

5TH GRADE • ENGLISH

In poetry, how many lines are in a sonnet?

5TH GRADE • EARTH SCIENCE

Which type of rock is most commonly found buried deep under mountains or in the Earth's crust?

○ A. Igneous ○ C. Metamorphic

○ B. Sedimentary ○ D. Seismic

$1,000,000 Question

5TH GRADE • WORLD HISTORY

Approximately when were the first coins minted?

○ A. 800 B.C. ○ C. 32 B.C.

○ B. 800 A.D. ○ D. 400 B.C.

QUIZ NUMBER 25

(chalkboard notes: WHAT STAR IS CLOSEST TO EARTH? · =9 16 25 36 49 64)

1ST GRADE ▪ SPELLING & GRAMMAR

Spell the plural of the noun *tooth*.

1ST GRADE ▪ SCIENCE

Every magnet has its own magnetic _____.

○ A. Spin   ○ C. Field

○ B. Movement   ○ D. Hard drive

2ND GRADE ▪ SOCIAL STUDIES

Which elected officials are also known as "lawmakers"?

2ND GRADE ▪ ASTRONOMY

The constellation of stars that resemble a flying horse is known as _____.

3RD GRADE ▪ MATH

$6.74 - 3 =$ _____.

3RD GRADE ▪ GEOGRAPHY

The ancient city of Constantinople is today known as _____.

○ A. Beirut   ○ C. New Delhi

○ B. Istanbul   ○ D. Baghdad

4TH GRADE ▪ SPELLING

In the world of cosmetics, spell the kind of makeup that goes on the eyelashes.

4TH GRADE ▪ GRAMMAR

Which two words are homonyms?

- ○ A. Blue and blew
- ○ B. White and black
- ○ C. Large and big
- ○ D. Chip and dip

5TH GRADE ▪ ASTRONOMY

If an orbit around the sun is not quite round, it is called _____.

5TH GRADE ▪ COMPUTERS

What does CPU stand for?

$1,000,000 Question

5TH GRADE ▪ MUSIC

Which is not a stringed instrument?

- ○ A. Zither
- ○ B. Concertina
- ○ C. Tambura
- ○ D. Lute

Where the Bard Went to the Board . . .
William Shakespeare, who would go on to write 37 of the most famous plays in history, attended 5th grade around 1575 at the Stratford Grammar School in Stratford-on-Avon, England.

1ST GRADE ▪ ENGLISH

Where would you put the comma in the following sentence? "I bought pears apples and bananas."

1ST GRADE ▪ SOCIAL STUDIES

On the back of the U.S. penny, there is a picture of
_____.

2ND GRADE ▪ SCIENCE

How long does it take for Earth to complete one rotation around its axis?

2ND GRADE ▪ MEASUREMENTS

How many meters are in a kilometer?

3RD GRADE ▪ WORLD GEOGRAPHY

What is the capital of Australia?

○ A. Sydney   ○ C. Canberra

○ B. Melbourne   ○ D. Perth

3RD GRADE ▪ U.S. HISTORY

In the U.S., the Bill of Rights guarantees that citizens will have _____.

○ A. Jobs   ○ C. Personal freedoms

○ B. An army   ○ D. Health benefits

A heptagon is a shape with how many sides?

Which two words are synonyms?

○ A. Step and stride

○ C. Learn and burn

○ B. Tall and short

○ D. Boy and buoy

Nicolaus Copernicus is known as the Father of Modern _____.

○ A. Physics

○ C. Zoology

○ B. Geometry

○ D. Astronomy

What does RAM stand for?

$1,000,000 Question

What was the name of the ship of the explorer Captain James Cook?

Dominique Moceanu, from Hollywood, California, won her first gymnastics gold medal at the U.S. Championships when she was only ten years old. By the time she was fourteen in 1996, she was an Olympic champion and had published her autobiography.

QUIZ NUMBER 27

1ST GRADE ▪ SPELLING

Spell the missing word: "The response to the question is the _____."

1ST GRADE ▪ U.S. GEOGRAPHY

What U.S. treasure is in New York Harbor?

2ND GRADE ▪ MEASUREMENTS

How many gallons are in 12 quarts?

2ND GRADE ▪ U.S. HISTORY

Who runs the executive branch of the U.S. government?

- ○ A. The chief justice
- ○ B. The attorney general
- ○ C. The president
- ○ D. The speaker of the house

3RD GRADE ▪ MATH

What is the name of a figure with eight sides?

3RD GRADE ▪ SCIENCE

What gas makes the bubbles in a soft drink?

- ○ A. Oxygen
- ○ B. Nitrogen
- ○ C. Methane
- ○ D. Carbon dioxide

What is the northernmost country in Africa?

Who was the first man to successfully climb to the peak of Mount Everest?

Who wrote *Tom Sawyer*?

What is another name for a deep sea hydrothermal vent?

$1,000,000 Question

Which of these was invented first?

- ○ A. Instant coffee
- ○ B. The Band-Aid
- ○ C. The modern zipper
- ○ D. Stainless steel

The Pot of Gold Is Literacy . . . Since 1983 the Public Broadcasting System has been doing its share to help kids learn how to read with their show *Reading Rainbow*. The show's slogan is "Opening Books, Opening Minds."

1ST GRADE ▪ PHYS. ED.

What is it called when a baseball team in the field gets two outs on the same play?

1ST GRADE ▪ ANIMAL SCIENCE

❏ **True** ❏ **False**

A mouse is a mammal.

2ND GRADE ▪ U.S. GEOGRAPHY

What U.S. city features a huge arch known as the "Gateway to the West"?

2ND GRADE ▪ ANIMAL SCIENCE

❏ **True** ❏ **False**

The Green Iguana eats mostly small animals.

3RD GRADE ▪ MATH

What distinguishes an isosceles triangle from other triangles?

3RD GRADE ▪ HEALTH

Who proved that germs cause diseases?

○ A. Marie Curie ○ C. Albert Einstein

○ B. Louis Pasteur ○ D. Nunzio Bacteri

4TH GRADE ▪ LITERATURE

Spell—but do not speak—the last name of Harry Potter's arch-enemy.

4TH GRADE ▪ U.S. HISTORY

Who invented bifocal eyeglasses?

5TH GRADE ▪ HEALTH

The three main types of food are carbohydrates, proteins and _____.

5TH GRADE ▪ COMPUTER

When was the first large-scale electronic computer built?

○ A. 1917   ○ C. 1977

○ B. 1946   ○ D. 1965

$1,000,000 Question

5TH GRADE ▪ ASTRONOMY

Pluto is _____ times farther from the Sun than the Earth.

○ A. 4   ○ C. 400

○ B. 40   ○ D. 4,000

Rock Around the Clock . . . 5th grader Ben Weymiller of Tacoma, Washington, held his own "Rock-a-thon" event and started his own website to raise money for the Bridge Children's Hospital. Ben thought there weren't enough rocking chairs in the hospital for parents and nurses to rock the sick kids—so he took care of it.

1ST GRADE ▪ GRAMMAR

Which word in the following sentence is a contraction? "I wanted to, but my mom says I can't go."

1ST GRADE ▪ MATH

❏ **True** ❏ **False**

(3×4) is the same as $(3 \times 3 \times 3 \times 3)$.

2ND GRADE ▪ MEASUREMENTS

What is the approximate diameter of a dime?

○ A. 1.7 millimeters ○ C. 1.7 meters

○ B. 1.7 centimeters ○ D. 1.7 kilometers

2ND GRADE ▪ WORLD GEOGRAPHY

What ocean lies between Africa and South America?

3RD GRADE ▪ ANIMAL SCIENCE

On what continent would you be most apt to encounter a jaguar in the wild?

○ A. North America ○ C. Africa

○ B. South America ○ D. Asia

Spell the first name of Harry Potter's closest female friend.

Which U.S. president resigned?

Although he painted in a variety of styles, Pablo Picasso is best known for his _____ paintings.

○ A. Impressionistic   ○ C. Realistic

○ B. Cubist   ○ D. Romantic

Who was the first man to orbit the Earth in space?

In what century was the French Revolution?

$1,000,000 Question

Name the four U.S. presidents who were assassinated.

The Starting-Early Award goes to Pablo Picasso, who got a head start on the competition on his way to becoming the most famous artist of the 20th century. His famous painting *Picador* was finished when Pablo was just 8 years old.

1ST GRADE ▪ LITERATURE

How does Dorothy get to Oz?

1ST GRADE ▪ U.S. HISTORY

Which U.S. war was fought between the North and the South?

2ND GRADE ▪ ASTRONOMY

In which galaxy is our sun?

2ND GRADE ▪ PHYS. ED.

Which two games use the same ball?

○ A. Baseball and softball   ○ C. Soccer and volleyball

○ B. Dodgeball and kickball   ○ D. Tennis and handball

3RD GRADE ▪ MATH

$7/8 - 3/4 = $ _____.

3RD GRADE ▪ PHYS. ED.

Which are the most similar?

○ A. Sit-ups and push-ups

○ B. Pull-ups and chin-ups

○ C. Squat thrusts and jumping jacks

○ D. Deep-knee bends and touch-your-toes

4th Grade ▪ Geography

What is the southernmost U.S. state?

4th Grade ▪ World History

Who is known as "The Father of Modern India"?

5th Grade ▪ Geometry

Which is true of a 120-degree angle?

○ A. It is acute.   ○ C. It is obtuse.

○ B. It is right.   ○ D. It is straight.

5th Grade ▪ Astronomy

The great scientist Galileo was born in which year A.D.?

○ A. 1464   ○ C. 1664

○ B. 1564   ○ D. 1764

$1,000,000 Question

5th Grade ▪ Earth Science

Who discovered that electricity could be made to flow through a wire by passing the wire between the poles of a magnet?

Didja Know . . . Ruth Lawrence was the youngest student to enter Oxford University. She matriculated at age 11.

QUIZ NUMBER 31

1ST GRADE • SCIENCE

Which won't an herbivore eat?

- ○ A. Salad
- ○ B. Vegetables
- ○ C. Carrots
- ○ D. Steak

1ST GRADE • EARTH SCIENCE

What common substance found on the surface of the Earth is melted to make glass?

2ND GRADE • MATH

Express $\frac{1}{5}$ as a percentage.

2ND GRADE • U.S. HISTORY

What was the last name of the U.S. president whose first name was Millard?

3RD GRADE • WORLD HISTORY

On what continent did Genghis Khan build his empire?

3RD GRADE • U.S. GEOGRAPHY

What river flows through the Grand Canyon?

Which is the second planet from the Sun?

On the periodic table, what element is represented by the letter B?

Which type of dance requires music that is three beats to the measure?

○ A. Tango   ○ C. Break-dancing

○ B. Waltz   ○ D. Fox trot

Who wrote *To Kill A Mockingbird*?

○ A. Truman Capote   ○ C. John Steinbeck

○ B. Ernest Hemingway   ○ D. Harper Lee

$1,000,000 Question

Who designed the first atomic reactor?

Sibling String Section . . . Jessica Constant and her two siblings were well-known classical musicians who had played at the Kennedy Center in Washington, D.C., by the time they were out of grade school. Brothers Pierre and Daniel are violinists, while Jessica is a cellist. Her advice to young people, "Be a student first."

1ST GRADE ▪ PHYS. ED.

In which sport do you break the rules by "walking"?

○ A. Baseball ○ C. Football

○ B. Soccer ○ D. Basketball

1ST GRADE ▪ ANIMAL SCIENCE

What is the tallest animal?

2ND GRADE ▪ ENGLISH

How many proper nouns are in the following sentence? "Mary and Bill drove through Kansas without stopping the car."

2ND GRADE ▪ WORLD GEOGRAPHY

On which continent is Kenya?

3RD GRADE ▪ PHYSICS

Which changes a sound's pitch?

○ A. Volume ○ C. Wavelength

○ B. Echo ○ D. Squelch

3RD GRADE ▪ HUMAN SCIENCE

❑ True ❑ False

The human shoulder is an example of a ball-and-socket joint.

Following World War II, what European city was divided in two by a wall?

In the northern hemisphere, in what month is the autumnal equinox?

Which of the following is a compound word?

- ○ A. Moonbeam
- ○ B. Almanac
- ○ C. Ocean
- ○ D. Poetry

Who wrote *The Old Man and the Sea*?

- ○ A. John Steinbeck
- ○ B. Norman Mailer
- ○ C. Jack Kerouac
- ○ D. Ernest Hemingway

$1,000,000 Question

If $15y = 5x$, what must be true:

- ○ A. $3y = x$
- ○ B. $y = 2/x$
- ○ C. $y = x/2$
- ○ D. $y = 3x$

5th Grade Inspiration . . . Kentucky 5th grader Arbella Sawyer was diagnosed with rheumatoid arthritis when she was 6. As an inspiration to others who suffer from the same disease, Arbella bravely leads each year's local Arthritis Walk.

1ST GRADE ▪ ENGLISH

What's a limerick?

1ST GRADE ▪ ANIMAL SCIENCE

What is, by far, the most numerous of the animal species?

○ A. Reptiles ○ C. Insects

○ B. Mammals ○ D. Fish

2ND GRADE ▪ MATH

One fourth of 36 is _____.

2ND GRADE ▪ U.S. HISTORY

What was the last name of the U.S. president whose first name was Chester?

3RD GRADE ▪ PHYS. ED.

❑ **True** ❑ **False**

A squat thrust involves kicking your legs out behind you.

3RD GRADE ▪ WORLD HISTORY

Who was the first European to journey to China?

4TH GRADE ▪ SOCIAL STUDIES

In the phrase "pop music," what is pop short for?

○ A. Soda pop
○ B. Popular
○ C. Finger popping
○ D. Popcorn

4TH GRADE ▪ HEALTH

In the sleep cycle REM, which part of your body moves quickly?

5TH GRADE ▪ SPELLING

Heat rays are also known as _____.

○ A. Infrared Rays
○ B. Microwaves
○ C. Laser Beams
○ D. Sine Waves

5TH GRADE ▪ ART

Which artist painted his most famous paintings in Tahiti?

○ A. Pablo Picasso
○ B. Claude Monet
○ C. Paul Gauguin
○ D. Henri de Toulouse-
Lautrec

$1,000,000 Question

5TH GRADE ▪ ANIMAL SCIENCE

What is the world's deadliest snake?

5th Grade Heroes . . . In 2005, 5th grader Trey Romero of Biloxi, Mississippi, was boating with his father when they witnessed a boating accident. When his father jumped overboard to save those who were injured, Trey safely piloted their boat back to dock!

WHAT STAR IS CLOSEST TO EARTH?

QUIZ NUMBER 34

1ST GRADE ▪ PHYS. ED.

Which are two names for the same track-and-field event?

○ A. Pole vault and high jump

○ B. Long jump and broad jump

○ C. Shot put and hammer throw

○ D. Triple jump and high hurdles

1ST GRADE ▪ U.S. GEOGRAPHY

What is the northernmost U.S. state?

2ND GRADE ▪ MATH

What is one-sixth of 72?

2ND GRADE ▪ ENGLISH

How many verbs are there in the following sentence? "I am the leader, so do your work."

3RD GRADE ▪ EARTH SCIENCE

Where is air pressure greater, at the Earth's surface or far up in the sky?

3RD GRADE ▪ GEOMETRY

❏ **True**   ❏ **False**

You determine the area of a polygon by adding up the lengths of its sides.

4TH GRADE ▪ SOCIAL STUDIES

❏ **True**   ❏ **False**

There are more people living today in Los Angeles than there were in the world back in the Stone Age.

4TH GRADE ▪ U.S. HISTORY

What was driven into the ground to celebrate the completion of North America's first transcontinental railroad?

5TH GRADE ▪ WORLD GEOGRAPHY

Portugal borders Spain on one side and _____ on the other.

5TH GRADE ▪ HEALTH

What hormone do diabetics take to help them regulate their blood-sugar level?

$1,000,000 Question

5TH GRADE ▪ U.S. HISTORY

Which U.S. president started the baseball tradition known as the "7th inning stretch"?

1ST GRADE ▪ ENGLISH

In the nursery rhyme, who jumped over the candlestick?

1ST GRADE ▪ PHYS. ED.

Crunches exercise what part of your body?

2ND GRADE ▪ U.S. GEOGRAPHY

What river flows through New Orleans, Louisiana?

2ND GRADE ▪ ASTRONOMY

How long does it take Earth to completely orbit the Sun?

3RD GRADE ▪ VOCABULARY

When you make something more concentrated, do you make it stronger or weaker?

3RD GRADE ▪ BIOLOGY

In the human body, which system is the heart in?

○ A. Respiratory   ○ C. Circulatory

○ B. Digestive   ○ D. Nervous

4TH GRADE ▪ GRAMMAR

How many articles are found in the following sentence? "The rabbit jumped into the hole."

4TH GRADE ▪ WORLD HISTORY

What type of government did the Soviet Union have?

5TH GRADE ▪ ASTRONOMY

How many moons does Venus have?

5TH GRADE ▪ MUSIC

Which of the following woodwind instruments is the largest?

○ A. Piccolo   ○ C. Recorder

○ B. Clarinet   ○ D. Oboe

$1,000,000 Question

5TH GRADE ▪ ART

The paintings of Salvador Dalí are examples of what school of art?

○ A. Realist   ○ C. Impressionist

○ B. Surrealist   ○ D. Abstract

Inspiration . . . The county executive in the Spokane, Washington, area is Ron Sims, who says he was inspired to achieve by his 5th grade teacher Ronald Miller, who taught him to have confidence in himself and have faith in his ability.

1ST GRADE ▪ ENGLISH

How many adjectives are in the following sentence?
"The principal is a beautiful woman."

1ST GRADE ▪ SOCIAL STUDIES

How much money is "two bits"?

2ND GRADE ▪ WORLD HISTORY

The ancient Roman empire was based on which continent?

2ND GRADE ▪ MEASUREMENTS

How many grams are in a kilogram?

3RD GRADE ▪ MATH

$9 \times 30 \times 100 =$ _____.

3RD GRADE ▪ ANIMAL SCIENCE

Which grouping has the most animals in it?

- ○ A. A genus
- ○ B. A kingdom
- ○ C. A species
- ○ D. A klotch

4TH GRADE · EARTH SCIENCE

A potato is also a _____.

- ○ A. Seed
- ○ B. Nut
- ○ C. Tuber
- ○ D. Stem

4TH GRADE · U.S. HISTORY

Translated into English, what does Puerto Rico mean?

- ○ A. Red door
- ○ B. Rich port
- ○ C. Sandy island
- ○ D. Palm-tree paradise

5TH GRADE · PHYSICAL SCIENCE

Which is an example of a simple machine?

- ○ A. Volcano
- ○ B. Computer
- ○ C. Steam engine
- ○ D. Pulley

5TH GRADE · WORLD GEOGRAPHY

What mountain range lies between France and Spain?

$1,000,000 Question

5TH GRADE · U.S. GEOGRAPHY

Which U.S. state is known as the "North Star State"?

- ○ A. Wisconsin
- ○ B. Alaska
- ○ C. Washington
- ○ D. Minnesota

1st Grade ▪ Spelling

Spell the missing word: The Rockies are a range of
_____.

1st Grade ▪ Social Studies

In what century did Samuel Morse invent the
telegraph?

2nd Grade ▪ Animal Science

❑ **True** ❑ **False**

The raccoon is a marsupial.

2nd Grade ▪ Phys. Ed.

Which of the following is not a track-and-field event?

○ A. Pole vault ○ C. Hammer throw

○ B. Mile run ○ D. Individual medley

3rd Grade ▪ Math

What is the place value of the 7 in 743,541?

3rd Grade ▪ Earth Science

Limestone, sandstone and gypsum are examples of
what type of rock?

○ A. Igneous   ○ C. Sedimentary

○ B. Metamorphic   ○ D. Ledge

4TH GRADE ▪ WORLD GEOGRAPHY

What is the longest river in Europe?

○ A. Volga   ○ C. Bosphorus

○ B. Danube   ○ D. Seine

4TH GRADE ▪ WORLD HISTORY

To the ancient Egyptians, what primary purpose did the pyramids serve?

○ A. Observation posts   ○ C. Royal tombs

○ B. Landmarks for travelers   ○ D. Royal palaces

4TH GRADE ▪ ENGLISH

Which pair of words are antonyms?

○ A. Windy and dry   ○ C. Agony and ecstasy

○ B. Rain and reign   ○ D. Quantum and quark

5TH GRADE ▪ ASTRONOMY

What U.S. space program sent astronauts into space in pairs?

$1,000,000 Question

5TH GRADE ▪ HISTORY

Which of these was invented first?

○ A. TV   ○ C. Lie detector

○ B. Frozen food   ○ D. Pop-up toaster

1st Grade ▪ Dance

What type of dancing involves wearing special shoes with metal plates on the bottom?

1st Grade ▪ Animal Science

❑ **True**   ❑ **False**

Some mammals breathe through gills.

2nd Grade ▪ Social Studies

Which is not a valid reason to build a dam?

○ A. To make a reservoir   ○ C. To attract beavers

○ B. To irrigate land   ○ D. To make electricity

2nd Grade ▪ Animal Science

What is the fastest land animal?

3rd Grade ▪ Math

Which type of angle describes the corner of a square?

○ A. Acute angle   ○ C. Right angle

○ B. Obtuse angle   ○ D. Complimentary angle

3rd Grade ▪ World Geography

On which continent is the nation of Cameroon?

There is a human organ that comes in pairs, is shaped like a bean, and cleans the blood. What is it? Please spell your answer.

In what U.S. city was Martin Luther King assassinated in 1968?

What is a radio detecting and ranging machine better known as?

Who wrote the science-fiction novel *The Time Machine*?

$1,000,000 Question

Spell the name of the dinosaur that could fly.

A Tip for Parents . . . According to the experts at www.familyeducation.com, you should participate in your child's education on a nightly basis. Browse frequently assigned topics and get quick facts in math, science, English, geography, history, and social studies. Use them to quiz your child.

1st Grade • English

Which of the following words is *not* a contraction?

- ○ A. Won't
- ○ B. We'll
- ○ C. Cannot
- ○ D. I'm

1st Grade • Phys. Ed.

In baseball, how many outs does the team in the field need to make before they get a turn at bat?

2nd Grade • Math

One-fifth of 15 equals _____.

2nd Grade • Math

What is the total number of dots on a pair of dice?

3rd Grade • Social Studies

When prices go up, it is called _____.

- ○ A. Taxation
- ○ B. Deflation
- ○ C. Inflation
- ○ D. Stagflation

3rd Grade • Animal Science

❑ True   ❑ False

A porcupine's quills are really its hair.

4TH GRADE ▪ U.S. HISTORY

Who shot President John F. Kennedy?

4TH GRADE ▪ ART

The earliest known paintings were found painted on

_____.

○ A. Floors of buildings ○ C. Clay tablets

○ B. Parchment ○ D. Cave walls

5TH GRADE ▪ SPELLING

Spell the process of moving water from lakes or rivers to the desert so that crops can be grown and communities built.

5TH GRADE ▪ ANIMAL SCIENCE

Invertebrate animals have no _____.

○ A. Legs ○ C. Spine

○ B. Tail ○ D. Bladder

$1,000,000 Question

5TH GRADE ▪ WORLD GEOGRAPHY

What was the country of Iran known as 2,000 years ago?

Yeah, but Can He Spell It Backward? . . .
The 2005 National Spelling Bee was won by
Anurag Kashyap of San Diego, California. He
won by correctly spelling *appoggiatura*. That's
a musical term for a really, really small note.

1st Grade ▪ Science

Which does not have cells?

○ A. Human being   ○ C. Onion skin

○ B. Maple leaf   ○ D. Granite

1st Grade ▪ Arithmetic

❏ **True**   ❏ **False**

You can put 23 chairs in six even rows of four.

2nd Grade ▪ Vocabulary

Precipitation is the same as _____.

○ A. Sunburn   ○ C. Wind

○ B. Low pressure   ○ D. Rain

2nd Grade ▪ Animal Science

In which state are you most apt to see an alligator?

○ A. Maine   ○ C. Montana

○ B. Florida   ○ D. Arizona

3rd Grade ▪ U.S. History

Which U.S. president served the longest?

3rd Grade ▪ Biology

How many stomachs does a cow have?

○ A. 1   ○ C. 3

○ B. 2   ○ D. 4

4th Grade ▪ U.S. Geography

The state of Kentucky lies just to the west of what mountain range?

4th Grade ▪ Earth Science

Name four cardinal directions.

5th Grade ▪ Social Studies

Who is the only U.S. president to have been divorced?

5th Grade ▪ World History

What explorer introduced tobacco smoking to the English?

$1,000,000 Question

5th Grade ▪ Art

What country was the painter Rembrandt from?

Are You Sure That's Not Paint-By-Numbers? Now 12 years old, the gifted painter named Akiane has been creating masterworks since she was 8. Not yet a teenager, she has been named one of the 20 most accomplished visual artists in the world.

QUIZ NUMBER 41

1ST GRADE ▪ U.S. GEOGRAPHY

What is the country just south of Texas?

1ST GRADE ▪ SCIENCE

A horse belongs to the animal class known as

_____.

2ND GRADE ▪ GRAMMAR

How many adjectives are there in this sentence?
"My brown dog grabbed the bleached bone in his
wet mouth."

2ND GRADE ▪ HEALTH

What type of food is wheat?

- ○ A. Fruit
- ○ B. Vegetable
- ○ C. Grain
- ○ D. Granola

3RD GRADE ▪ SPELLING

Spell the word that goes in the blank: "My favorite
Shakespeare play is *Romeo and* _____."

3RD GRADE ▪ DANCE

What is the name of the Spanish dance that involves
the stomping of the heels and clapping of the hands?

Which is the closest planet to the Sun?

On the periodic table, what element is represented by the letter H?

Which saxophone can play the lowest note?

○ A. Soprano ○ C. Alto

○ B. Baritone ○ D. Tenor

What is the hard shell on the outside of an ant's body called?

$1,000,000 Question

What geologic era are we in right now?

**Smart Kids Make Smart Grown-Ups . . .
Brian Greene could multiply 30-digit
numbers in his head while still a kid and,
as an adult, became a well-known physicist.**

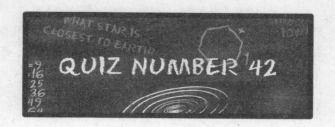

QUIZ NUMBER 42

1st Grade · Phys. Ed.

Which sport features no time clock?

- ○ A. Baseball
- ○ B. Basketball
- ○ C. Football
- ○ D. Hockey

1st Grade · Social Studies

In what month do Americans celebrate Independence Day?

2nd Grade · History

What were the names of Christopher Columbus's ships in 1492?

2nd Grade · World Geography

On which continent is Mongolia?

3rd Grade · Animal Science

What is the slowest land mammal?

3rd Grade · Human Science

❏ True   ❏ False

The hyoid bone is in your wrist.

4TH GRADE ▪ U.S. GEOGRAPHY

In terms of surface area, what is the smallest of the Great Lakes?

4TH GRADE ▪ MEASUREMENTS & MATH

How many seconds are there in an hour?

5TH GRADE ▪ U.S. HISTORY

❑ True   ❑ False

There were no pigs in North America until they were brought over from Europe by settlers.

5TH GRADE ▪ MATH

What is the height of a triangle that has a base three inches long and an area of 15 square inches?

$1,000,000 Question

5TH GRADE ▪ ART

The paintings of Claude Monet are examples of which school of art?

❍ A. Realism   ❍ C. Impressionism

❍ B. Romanticism   ❍ D. Abstract

> **A Genius Among Geniuses . . . Though the measuring of IQ is an inexact science, according to the Guinness Book of World Records the smartest person in the world is Marilyn vos Savant, a writer who is married to Robert Jarvik, who invented the artificial heart. With brain power like that you could light up a small city.**

1ST GRADE ▪ SPELLING

Spell the word that means the opposite of full.

1ST GRADE ▪ ANIMAL SCIENCE

Walruses are most apt to be found . . .

○ A. Near Antarctica.   ○ C. Near Australia.

○ B. Near South America.   ○ D. Near the North Pole.

2ND GRADE ▪ ANIMAL SCIENCE

❏ **True**   ❏ **False**

Crabs live only in the ocean.

2ND GRADE ▪ SPELLING

Spell the sport that Michael Jordan played.

3RD GRADE ▪ WORLD GEOGRAPHY

What is the capital of Italy?

3RD GRADE ▪ HEALTH

Which of the following is caused by a virus?

○ A. Sunburn   ○ C. Mumps

○ B. Cramps   ○ D. Cataracts

4TH GRADE ▪ MATH

A polygon must have more than _____ sides.

4TH GRADE ▪ ENGLISH

In the Washington Irving story, what war takes place while Rip Van Winkle is asleep?

5TH GRADE ▪ MATH

What whole number is closest to the square root of 99?

5TH GRADE ▪ SOCIAL STUDIES

If a nation's economy is agrarian, it makes money through _____.

○ A. Importing   ○ C. Farms

○ B. Factories   ○ D. Technology

$1,000,000 Question

5TH GRADE ▪ ANIMAL SCIENCE

❑ True   ❑ False

The bumblebee bat is extinct.

> **Schoolhouse Rock . . . During the 1970s millions of children learned math, history and science lessons on Saturday morning TV by watching short cartoons that turned each lesson into an animated rock video.**

1ST GRADE ▪ LITERATURE

The Grinch lives on the outskirts of what town?

1ST GRADE ▪ U.S. GEOGRAPHY

What four U.S. states border Mexico?

2ND GRADE ▪ WORLD GEOGRAPHY

❑ True   ❑ False

Mexico is in the southern hemisphere.

2ND GRADE ▪ SPELLING

The North Pole is covered by a frozen sea. Spell the name of that sea.

3RD GRADE ▪ ASTRONOMY

❑ True   ❑ False

A blue giant star is hotter than a red dwarf star.

3RD GRADE ▪ ANIMAL SCIENCE

Where do most crustaceans live?

   ○ A. Mountains   ○ C. Ocean

   ○ B. Rain forest   ○ D. Desert

4TH GRADE • MATH

If the airport runway is 3,000 yards long and 20 yards wide, how many square yards in size is it?

4TH GRADE • PHYS. ED.

Aerobics exercises will not . . .

○ A. Improve breathing. ○ C. Burn calories.

○ B. Strengthen the heart. ○ D. Build big muscles.

5TH GRADE • U.S. HISTORY

Teddy Roosevelt said, "Talk softly and carry a big _____."

5TH GRADE • WORLD HISTORY

Who was emperor of the Roman Empire when Rome burned in 64 A.D.?

$1,000,000 Question

5TH GRADE • ASTRONOMY

In Earth time, about how long does it take Saturn to orbit once around the Sun?

○ A. 3 years ○ C. 300 years

○ B. 30 years ○ D. 3,000 years

Great Teacher! Annie Sullivan earned her reputation as an expert educator by teaching the blind and deaf Helen Keller how to read, write and speak. She is the title figure in the award-winning play and film *The Miracle Worker*.

1ST GRADE ▪ ENGLISH

In the nursery rhyme, what was it that Jack Spratt could not eat?

1ST GRADE ▪ ANIMAL SCIENCE

What's the largest type of bear?

2ND GRADE ▪ EARTH SCIENCE

❑ **True**   ❑ **False**

Cirrus clouds are usually higher in the sky than cumulus clouds.

2ND GRADE ▪ SOCIAL STUDIES

Which is the only one of the Seven Wonders of the Ancient World to still stand?

3RD GRADE ▪ MATH

There are five groups of students. Each group had 34 pupils. How many students are there all together?

3RD GRADE ▪ U.S. GEOGRAPHY

Which state is farther west, Montana or Arkansas?

4TH GRADE ▪ EARTH SCIENCE

In North America, the watershed that separates the waters that drain into the Atlantic Ocean from those that drain into the Pacific is called the _____.

4TH GRADE ▪ U.S. GEOGRAPHY

What is the capital of Tennessee?

5TH GRADE ▪ ASTRONOMY

How many known moons does Jupiter have?

○ A. 11   ○ C. 63

○ B. 59   ○ D. 68

5TH GRADE ▪ SOCIAL STUDIES

Which country is named after the family that rules it?

○ A. Morocco   ○ C. Sudan

○ B. Monaco   ○ D. Saudi Arabia

$1,000,000 Question

5TH GRADE ▪ LITERATURE

Who wrote *Ivanhoe*?

Work to Do . . . Despite the fact that every country tries as hard as it can to educate its children, one third of the world's kids cannot read or write.

QUIZ NUMBER 46

1st Grade ▪ English

Where is the mistake in the following sentence?
"I have one fish, too turtles, and three puppies."

1st Grade ▪ Phys. Ed.

Name two ways to knock an opponent out of a
dodge ball game.

2nd Grade ▪ Animal Science

❑ **True**   ❑ **False**

The last Komodo Dragon died in captivity in the late
nineteenth century.

2nd Grade ▪ Measurements

How many pecks are in a bushel?

3rd Grade ▪ U.S. History

What was the capital of the Union side during the
Civil War?

3rd Grade ▪ World Geography

In which part of the world would you be most apt to
find a tundra?

○ A. Equator   ○ C. Mountains

○ B. Tropics   ○ D. Arctic

4TH GRADE ▪ SOCIAL STUDIES

The popular type of food known as sushi originated in which country?

- ◯ A. China
- ◯ B. Japan
- ◯ C. Mongolia
- ◯ D. The Philippines

4TH GRADE ▪ U.S. GEOGRAPHY

In what U.S. state is Yosemite National Park?

5TH GRADE ▪ ART

Which artist painted in the pop art genre?

- ◯ A. Keith Haring
- ◯ B. Jackson Pollock
- ◯ C. Andy Warhol
- ◯ D. Norman Rockwell

5TH GRADE ▪ LITERATURE

In what city does *The Hunchback of Notre Dame* take place?

$1,000,000 Question

5TH GRADE ▪ MATH

If $5y/3 = 20$, what does y equal?

Junior Bassmaster . . . Joey Nania, of Liberty Lake, Washington, won his first Junior Bass Fishing Championship when was in 5th grade. Today, at age sixteen, he auctions off personal appearances at fishing competitions and gives the money to charity.

1st-Grade ▪ Spelling

Spell the missing word: "BFF means Best _____ Forever!"

1st Grade ▪ Phys. Ed.

Name two ways to get a player out in kick ball.

2nd Grade ▪ Astronomy

When looking at the night sky, which planet appears brightest?

○ A. Venus   ○ C. Mars

○ B. Uranus   ○ D. Jupiter

2nd Grade ▪ Earth Science

❑ **True**   ❑ **False**

All snowflakes are crystals.

3rd Grade ▪ Math

What is 3 to the third power (3^3)?

3rd Grade ▪ Animal Science

Cotton comes from a plant. Silk comes from

_____ .

What is the longest river in Asia?

The founder of the colony of Pennsylvania was
_____.

Which boxing champ was stripped of his title because he refused to go into the U.S. Army?

Who was the only U.S. president to be sworn into office on an airplane?

$1,000,000 Question

Which of these was invented first?

- ○ A. Jet engine
- ○ C. Bubble gum
- ○ B. Electron microscope
- ○ D. Scotch tape

Reach for the Stars . . . When Becca Robison, of Ogden City, Utah, was in 5th grade she was already making plans for a space camp that would encourage young girls to become astronauts. Two years later she founded "Astrotots: Space Camp for Little Dippers."

QUIZ NUMBER 48

1ST GRADE • ASTRONOMY

If you count Pluto as a planet, how many planets are in our solar system?

1ST GRADE • ANIMAL SCIENCE

An example of an amphibian animal is a . . .

- ○ A. Human being
- ○ B. Horse
- ○ C. Lizard
- ○ D. Toad

2ND GRADE • PHYS. ED.

A soccer game takes place between two teams of (not counting substitutes) _____ players.

- ○ A. 9
- ○ B. 10
- ○ C. 11
- ○ D. 12

2ND GRADE • ANIMAL SCIENCE

On which continent is the cheetah's natural habitat?

3RD GRADE • MATH

How many degrees are in a circle?

3RD GRADE ▪ ASTRONOMY

Which is closest to true? The distance between the Earth and the Sun is _____ miles.

○ A. 96   ○ C. 96 million

○ B. 9.6 million   ○ D. 960 million

4TH GRADE ▪ LITERATURE

Who wrote the classic novel *Treasure Island*?

4TH GRADE ▪ WORLD GEOGRAPHY

In what country is the Taj Mahal?

5TH GRADE ▪ LITERATURE

Who wrote *Gulliver's Travels*?

5TH GRADE ▪ EARTH SCIENCE

Determining the size, depth, and distance of an object beneath the ocean by bouncing sound waves off of it is called _____.

$1,000,000 Question

5TH GRADE ▪ ANIMAL SCIENCE

Which organ in the body could be described as olfactory?

Exceptional 5th Graders . . . Juan Caramuel y Lobkowitz published astronomical tables at age 10.

1ST GRADE ▪ GRAMMAR

How many mistakes is in this sentence?

1ST GRADE ▪ ART

The world's oldest sculpture is in Egypt and appears to be guarding a pyramid. It's called the _____.

2ND GRADE ▪ ANIMAL SCIENCE

❑ **True**   ❑ **False**

The kiwi is a shy bird that cannot fly.

2ND GRADE ▪ ASTRONOMY

What was the name of the first man-made satellite to be put in orbit around the Earth?

3RD GRADE ▪ SOCIAL STUDIES

In what U.S. city is Mardi Gras celebrated?

3RD GRADE ▪ LIFE SCIENCE

In which system of the human body are the lungs?

○ A. Respiratory   ○ C. Circulatory

○ B. Digestive   ○ D. Nervous

4TH GRADE ▪ U.S. HISTORY

In what year did the Wright Brothers fly the first airplane?

4TH GRADE ▪ MATH

If a car is traveling 50 miles per hour, how long will it take for the car to go 225 miles?

5TH GRADE ▪ ART

During which period did Leonardo da Vinci live?

○ A. Dark Ages   ○ C. Medieval Times

○ B. Middle Ages   ○ D. the Renaissance

5TH GRADE ▪ LIFE SCIENCE

Which of these subatomic particles is neither positively nor negatively charged?

○ A. Proton   ○ C. Isotope

○ B. Electron   ○ D. Neutron

$1,000,000 Question

5TH GRADE ▪ WORLD GEOGRAPHY

Where is the country of Laos?

○ A. Southeast Asia   ○ C. Central Africa

○ B. The Middle East   ○ D. South America

Nature Lover . . . Eleven-year-old Will Schoenhals has spent 400 hours volunteering at the Three Forks Nature Center in Oklahoma's Sequoyah State Park.

1ST GRADE ▪ ANIMAL SCIENCE

❑ **True**   ❑ **False**

The Tyrannosaurus rex ate only plants.

1ST GRADE ▪ ENGLISH

How many nouns are there in the following sentence? "The horse ran into the barn and ate a lot of oats."

2ND GRADE ▪ MEASUREMENTS

What unit of measurement is abbreviated "qt."?

2ND GRADE ▪ GEOGRAPHY

Which continent is farthest south?

3RD GRADE ▪ EARTH SCIENCE

What U.S. city was largely destroyed by an earthquake in 1906?

3RD GRADE ▪ SOCIAL STUDIES

Which U.S. state produces the most citrus fruit?

4TH GRADE ▪ U.S. GEOGRAPHY

What is the capital of Virginia?

According to legend, what city suffered a major fire started by Mrs. O'Leary's cow?

In the name of the agency known as NASA what does the second A stand for?

Which pilot was the first to achieve supersonic flight?

$1,000,000 Question

5TH GRADE ▪ LITERATURE

In what future U.S. state did the character known as Zorro fight injustice?

Helping Others . . . John-Henry Lambin of Gardnerville, Nevada, was a 5th grader with asthma and dyslexia. Instead of letting his problems get him down he formed an organization called Kids Extreme to help other kids with problems achieve their goals.

1ST GRADE ▪ LITERATURE

In the book *Charlotte's Web*, what type of animal is Charlotte?

1ST GRADE ▪ WORLD GEOGRAPHY

In what country is the Great Wall?

2ND GRADE ▪ EARTH SCIENCE

The ocean current that runs northward along the eastern coast of the U.S. before turning eastward toward Europe is called the _____.

2ND GRADE ▪ PHYS. ED.

Which of the following is not a gymnastics event?

○ A. Balance beam   ○ C. Long jump

○ B. Rings   ○ D. Pommel horse

3RD GRADE ▪ U.S. GEOGRAPHY

In what U.S. state is the Grand Canyon?

3RD GRADE ▪ GEOMETRY

What kind of angle is a 90-degree angle?

What is the largest planet in the solar system?

On the periodic table, what letter represents potassium?

The slaves were freed during which war?

○ A. The Revolutionary War

○ B. The French and Indian War

○ C. The Civil War

○ D. The Great War

A bear's all-winter nap is called _____.
Please spell your answer.

$1,000,000 Question

Who revolutionized printing by inventing movable type?

Here She Comes—There She Goes . . . Sarah Chen of San Marino, California, at age 10, is a champion speed skater. She says, "My best advice to all my peers is to follow your dreams, never give up, and most of all have fun doing it!"

1st Grade • English

What is the conjunction in the following sentence?
"He thought he was smart but he was wrong."

1st Grade • U.S. History

In what year did man first walk on the Moon?

2nd Grade • Earth Science

Solar energy comes when _____ is used to produce electricity.

2nd Grade • World Geography

On which continent is Bosnia?

3rd Grade • World History

The Roman arena where gladiators fought was known as _____.

3rd Grade • Health

❑ **True**   ❑ **False**

Your scapula is in your shoulder.

4th Grade • U.S. Geography

In surface area, which is the largest of the Great Lakes?

4TH GRADE ▪ LIFE SCIENCE

The root of a hair is called the _____.

○ A. Nerve ending   ○ C. Capillary

○ B. Follicle   ○ D. Erector muscle

5TH GRADE ▪ LITERATURE

What is the name of the hero in the book *Holes*?

5TH GRADE ▪ BIOLOGY

Which is the part of your brain that allows you to think?

$1,000,000 Question

5TH GRADE ▪ U.S. HISTORY

What is the full name of the U.S. president who served the shortest term?

Teacher of the Year . . . In 1996, Leonard Swanton, a 5th grade teacher in Massachusetts' Lexington Public Schools was named the state's Teacher of the Year for his exceptional communication skills, and his ability to quietly yet forcefully relate his expectations to students.

QUIZ NUMBER 53

1st Grade ▪ World History

What was the name of the king and queen who financed Christopher Columbus's explorations?

1st Grade ▪ World Geography

What is the capital of Canada?

2nd Grade ▪ U.S. History

In what state was Abraham Lincoln born?

2nd Grade ▪ Social Studies

Who was the first person to fly alone and non-stop across the Atlantic Ocean?

3rd Grade ▪ Math

What is nine times thirteen?

3rd Grade ▪ English

How many adjectives are there in this sentence? "The brown fox ran hurriedly from the barking dogs, as the red sun rose in the East."

4th Grade ▪ Measurements

How many ounces are there in a pint?

Who wrote a series of books starring Henry Huggins and a dog named Ribsy?

What was the name of the first satellite to land on Mars?

Who wrote *The Charge of the Light Brigade?*

- ○ A. William Wordsworth
- ○ B. Alfred, Lord Tennyson
- ○ C. T.S. Eliot
- ○ D. Samuel Taylor Coleridge

$1,000,000 Question

The nation of Lesotho is completely surrounded by what other, larger country?

And the Gold Star Goes to . . . Meaghan Finn of Woburn, Massachusetts, who was only 10 years old when she led her community in a breast cancer walk to honor her neighbor. Meaghan raised $5,000.

1ST GRADE ▪ ART

What color must be mixed with the color of the clear sky to get the color of the grass?

1ST GRADE ▪ U.S. GEOGRAPHY

The capital of Hawaii is _____.

○ A. Waikiki   ○ C. Honolulu

○ B. Oahu   ○ D. Maui

2ND GRADE ▪ ENGLISH

How many adverbs in the following sentence? "He walked briskly through the forest as the wind smacked roughly into his face."

2ND GRADE ▪ WORLD GEOGRAPHY

What is the ocean between Africa and Australia called?

3RD GRADE ▪ ANIMAL SCIENCE

❑ **True**   ❑ **False**

Spiders are eight-legged insects.

3RD GRADE ▪ WORLD HISTORY

In what century did Marco Polo explore Asia?

○ A. 1200s ○ C. 1400s

○ B. 1300s ○ D. 1500s

4TH GRADE ▪ MATH

Which has a greater area? A square that is 30 feet by 30 feet, or a rectangle that is five feet by 200 feet.

4TH GRADE ▪ U.S. HISTORY

In what year did the stock market crash, starting the Great Depression?

5TH GRADE ▪ LITERATURE

What was the name of the *nice* teacher in Roald Dahl's book *Matilda*?

○ A. Miss Sugarpie ○ C. Miss Maple

○ B. Miss Honey ○ D. Miss Sweet 'N Low

5TH GRADE ▪ COMPUTER

On the Internet, Google is known as a _____.

$1,000,000 Question

5TH GRADE ▪ COMPUTERS

The resolution of a digital image is often measured in _____.

1ST GRADE • MUSIC

In the song "This Old Man," what does the old man give the dog?

1ST GRADE • SCIENCE

What tool is used to measure wind speed?

- ○ A. Hydrometer
- ○ B. Thermometer
- ○ C. Anamometer
- ○ D. Wind machine

2ND GRADE • MEASUREMENTS

Which has more days: March, April and May or September, October, and November?

2ND GRADE • EARTH SCIENCE

The amount of water in the air is called the

_____.

3RD GRADE • U.S. HISTORY

What was New York City known as in the year 1626?

3RD GRADE • ASTRONOMY

Which planet has a huge storm on its surface resembling an eye?

4TH GRADE ▪ U.S. GEOGRAPHY

What is the capital of West Virginia?

4TH GRADE ▪ U.S. HISTORY

What U.S. president preceded Franklin Roosevelt?

5TH GRADE ▪ SOCIAL STUDIES

In the federal agency known as the CIA, what does the I stand for?

5TH GRADE ▪ LITERATURE

Who wrote the poem *The Raven*?

$1,000,000 Question

5TH GRADE ▪ EARTH SCIENCE

In what month is the summer solstice if you're in Australia?

The Golden Brush Award Goes to . . .
British artist John Everett Millais, who
painted so well as a child that he entered
the Royal Academy of Arts at age 11.

1st Grade ▪ English

What are the nouns in the following sentence?
"My apple has a worm in it."

1st Grade ▪ History

Who was the first man to walk on the Moon?

2nd Grade ▪ World Geography

❏ **True**   ❏ **False**

The United States is in the western hemisphere.

2nd Grade ▪ Measurements

How many pints are in ten gallons?

3rd Grade ▪ U.S. History

In which war was Washington, D.C., attacked and the
White House burned?

3rd Grade ▪ Earth Science

Hydroelectric power is generated by what?

4TH GRADE ▪ MUSIC

The first operas were performed in which country?

○ A. France ○ C. Italy

○ B. Germany ○ D. England

4TH GRADE ▪ WORLD HISTORY

The ancient Olympics were held in which country?

○ A. Greece ○ C. Sparta

○ B. Troy ○ D. Constantinople

5TH GRADE ▪ SPELLING

Spell the name of the battle in which Napoleon Bonaparte met his final military defeat.

5TH GRADE ▪ MATH

If $y = 3x$ and $x = 9$, what does y equal?

$1,000,000 Question

5TH GRADE ▪ LITERATURE

Who wrote the *Iliad* and the *Odyssey*?

> **Computer Wiz . . . 5th grader Jacob Komar of Burlington, Connecticut, started a program called Computers for Communities. Being a "computer fanatic" he spent his spare time upgrading out-of-date computers and giving them to families in his community that couldn't afford one. His efforts earned him the Prudential Spirit of Community Award.**

1ST GRADE ▪ U.S. HISTORY

What was Johnny Appleseed famous for?

1ST GRADE ▪ SPELLING

Spell the missing word: "Her favorite dinosaur movie is _____ *Park*."

2ND GRADE ▪ ANIMAL SCIENCE

Where does ivory come from?

2ND GRADE ▪ SOCIAL STUDIES

What was the name of the dots-and-dashes system that enabled people to send and receive messages with a telegraph?

3RD GRADE ▪ EARTH SCIENCE

What is the only metal to be a liquid at normal temperatures?

3RD GRADE ▪ ASTRONOMY

About how far is Earth from the Moon?

   ○ A. 150,000 miles   ○ C. 250,000 miles

   ○ B. 25,000 miles   ○ D. 1 light year

What is the longest river in South America?

The email equivalent of junk mail is commonly called

_____.

In the name of the agency known as the FBI, spell the word beginning with the letter I.

What do we call a piece of art made up of small pieces of colored stone set into cement?

$1,000,000 Question

Which of these was invented last?

○ A. Computer   ○ C. Color TV

○ B. Ballpoint pen   ○ D. Helicopter

Prodigy Alert! Writer William Cullen Bryant first had his work published when he was 10.

1ST GRADE ▪ ENGLISH

In Mother Goose, the old woman who lived in a shoe had so many _____ she didn't know what to do.

1ST GRADE ▪ ANIMAL SCIENCE

The process of a tadpole developing into a frog is called _____.

○ A. Photosynthesis   ○ C. Osmosis

○ B. Homeostasis   ○ D. Metamorphosis

2ND GRADE ▪ EARTH SCIENCE

An oak-tree seed is sometimes called an _____.

2ND GRADE ▪ HEALTH

Technically, nuts are _____.

○ A. Meat   ○ C. Fruits

○ B. Vegetables ○ D. Grain

3RD GRADE ▪ MATH

❑ **True**   ❑ **False**

An equilateral triangle must be equiangular.

3RD GRADE ▪ ANIMAL SCIENCE

A caterpillar turns into a butterfly while encased in a
_____.

4TH GRADE ▪ SCIENCE

Charles Darwin is best known for his Theory of
_____.

○ A. Relativity   ○ C. Inertia

○ B. Evolution   ○ D. Gravitational Pull

4TH GRADE ▪ U.S. GEOGRAPHY

What is the capital of Georgia?

5TH GRADE ▪ U.S. HISTORY

Which U.S. president was never a general in the
army?

○ A. Grant   ○ C. Carter

○ B. Eisenhower   ○ D. Washington

5TH GRADE ▪ DANCE

What is a *pas de deux*?

$1,000,000 Question

5TH GRADE ▪ SOCIAL STUDIES

What is the state animal of West Virginia?

○ A. Red panda   ○ C. Raccoon

○ B. Black bear   ○ D. Opossum

1st Grade ▪ English

What is the symbol inside the parentheses called? (:)

1st Grade ▪ U.S. History

❑ **True**   ❑ **False**

Walt Disney invented cartoons.

2nd Grade ▪ Health

Gingivitis is also known as _____ disease.

2nd Grade ▪ Spelling

Which words in this sentence are misspelled?
"He was imediately greatful that the weather was glorious."

3rd Grade ▪ Science

The outermost layer of the Earth is called the
_____.

○ A. Upper mantle   ○ C. Soil

○ B. Lower mantle   ○ D. Crust

3rd Grade ▪ Math

What is the lowest prime number?

4TH GRADE ▪ U.S. HISTORY

In what year did the Lewis and Clark Expedition begin?

- ○ A. 1796
- ○ B. 1803
- ○ C. 1805
- ○ D. 1814

4TH GRADE ▪ WORLD GEOGRAPHY

Cyprus is an island in what sea?

5TH GRADE ▪ ENGLISH

In what century did poet Emily Dickinson live?

- ○ A. 17th
- ○ B. 18th
- ○ C. 19th
- ○ D. 20th

5TH GRADE ▪ SOCIAL STUDIES

In the name of the alliance known as NATO, what does the T stand for?

$1,000,000 Question

5TH GRADE ▪ MUSIC

To play a piece of music *allegro* means to play it
_____.

- ○ A. Using only sharp notes
- ○ B. At a varying tempo
- ○ C. Fast
- ○ D. Loud

Exceptional 5th Graders . . . Haley Joel Osment, who "saw dead people" in *The Sixth Sense* was nominated for the Best Supporting Actor Oscar at age 11.

QUIZ NUMBER 60

1st Grade ▪ Math

The answer to an addition problem is called the
_____.

1st Grade ▪ Science

Another word for a hurricane is a _____.

○ A. Tornado   ○ C. Water spout

○ B. Twister   ○ D. Cyclone

2nd Grade ▪ Health

To prevent tooth decay, what is added to our drinking
water?

2nd Grade ▪ Geography

In what state is Mount Rushmore?

3rd Grade ▪ Science

The center of the Earth is known as _____.

○ A. The lower mantle   ○ C. The eye

○ B. The epicenter   ○ D. The core

3rd Grade ▪ Earth Science

Plastic is made from _____.

○ A. Wood　　　　　○ C. Sand

○ B. Oil　　　　　　○ D. Rubber

4TH GRADE ▪ LITERATURE

Who wrote *Moby-Dick*?

4TH GRADE ▪ U.S. HISTORY

The first transcontinental railroad was completed in what year?

○ A. 1839　　　　　○ C. 1869

○ B. 1912　　　　　○ D. 1876

5TH GRADE ▪ WORLD HISTORY

Who was the leader of Italy during World War II?

5TH GRADE ▪ ANIMAL SCIENCE

What is the only mammal that also lays eggs?

$1,000,000 Question

5TH GRADE ▪ MATH

If 14y = 7x, which must be true?

○ A. x = y　　　　　○ C. x = y/2

○ B. y = x + 2　　　○ D. x = 2y

Most Students Award . . . Of American cities, New York City has the most 5th graders. All together there are more than a million students in the Big Apple. More than 100,000 are in the 5th grade!

1ST GRADE ▪ GEOGRAPHY

What is the capital of France?

1ST GRADE ▪ ART

How many crayons are in the deluxe box of Crayola Crayons?

2ND GRADE ▪ U.S. HISTORY

What is the last name of the U.S. president whose first name was Zachary?

2ND GRADE ▪ MUSIC

How many musicians play in a quintet?

3RD GRADE ▪ HEALTH

Which type of food would be best for you if you were on a low-sodium diet?

○ A. Low calorie   ○ C. Low salt

○ B. Low carb   ○ D. Sugar free

3RD GRADE ▪ ENGLISH

What is the symbol inside the parentheses called? (;)

What is it called when the Earth passes between the Moon and the Sun?

On the periodic table, what gas is represented by the letters "He"?

In what country is the city of Mecca?

In 1992, from which country did most U.S. immigrants come?

- ○ A. Germany
- ○ B. Ireland
- ○ C. Mexico
- ○ D. China

$1,000,000 Question

Who performed the first heart transplant in a human being?

And What Were You Doing at That Age? . . .
Jean Piaget, later a well-known psychologist,
published a paper on the albino sparrow at age 11.

1st Grade • Phys. Ed.

At what sport does Sasha Cohen excel?

- ○ A. Skiing
- ○ B. Speed skating
- ○ C. Figure skating
- ○ D. Ice hockey

1st Grade • Literature

What did the girls do when Georgie-Porgie kissed them?

2nd Grade • Math

If there are 11 questions per quiz in this book and 75 quizzes, how many questions are in this book?

2nd Grade • World Geography

On which continent is Norway?

3rd Grade • Social Studies

What was the name of the plane Charles Lindbergh flew across the Atlantic in 1927?

3rd Grade • Human Science

❏ **True**   ❏ **False**

Your coccyx (pronounced COX-six) is a small bone behind your sternum.

4TH GRADE ▪ GRAMMAR

Which of the following words is an adverb?

○ A. Jolly   ○ C. Quickly

○ B. Lonely   ○ D. Only

4TH GRADE ▪ U.S. GEOGRAPHY

What is the capital of Florida?

5TH GRADE ▪ LITERATURE

During what century did the poet Henry Wadsworth Longfellow live?

5TH GRADE ▪ PHYS. ED.

To the closest mile, how far is a marathon running race?

$1,000,000 Question

5TH GRADE ▪ ANIMAL SCIENCE

About how many years ago did the last woolly mammoths die out?

○ A. 300 years   ○ C. 30,000 years

○ B. 3,000 years   ○ D. 300,000 years

**The Doctor Who Couldn't Vote . . .
Balamurali Ambati graduated from
high school at 11, was a college junior
by age 12, and a doctor at 17.**

1st Grade ▪ Animal Science

☐ True ☐ False

A chimpanzee is a monkey.

1st Grade ▪ Music

The words of a song are sometimes called the

_____.

2nd Grade ▪ Astronomy

What animal does the constellation of stars named Leo resemble?

2nd Grade ▪ U.S. History

In what city was the U.S. Constitution signed?

3rd Grade ▪ Social Studies

Which is an important industry in West Virginia?

○ A. Pineapple farming ○ C. Coal mining

○ B. Gambling ○ D. Computer technology

3rd Grade ▪ Measurements

How many months are there in a century?

4TH GRADE ▪ MATH

If the diameter of a circle is 8 inches, what is the circle's radius?

4TH GRADE ▪ MUSIC

In what century did the first orchestras get together to play music?

5TH GRADE ▪ HUMAN SCIENCE

About how many different muscles are in the human body?

- ○ A. 50
- ○ B. 500
- ○ C. 5,000
- ○ D. 50,000

5TH GRADE ▪ MUSIC

What is the first name of the classical composer Mozart?

$1,000,000 Question

5TH GRADE ▪ ANIMAL SCIENCE

Name the three main parts of an ant's body.

> **5th Grade Heroes . . . Madison Valentine of Palo Alto, California, was having lunch with her 7-year-old brother Erickson when he began to choke on some grapes he had eaten. Luckily, Madison had just finished a Girl Scout first-aid class. She performed the Heimlich maneuver on her brother and saved his life.**

QUIZ NUMBER 64

1ST GRADE ▪ HEALTH

Bacteria is another word for . . .

○ A. Viruses.   ○ C. Disease.

○ B. Sickness.   ○ D. Germs.

1ST GRADE ▪ U.S. GEOGRAPHY

The Alamo is in which U.S. state?

2ND GRADE ▪ SCIENCE

The ocean's tides are caused by the _____.

○ A. Moon   ○ C. Sun

○ B. Wind   ○ D. Temperature

2ND GRADE ▪ U.S. HISTORY

Who is the head of the judicial branch of the U.S. government?

○ A. The chief justice

○ B. The attorney general

○ C. The president

○ D. The speaker of the House

3RD GRADE ▪ ANIMAL SCIENCE

Mother mammals feed their young with _____.

3RD GRADE • ENGLISH

What is the compound word in this sentence?
"The airport was crowded with panicky tourists
hurriedly moving from place to place."

4TH GRADE • GEOMETRY

An octagon is a shape with how many sides?

4TH GRADE • GRAMMAR

Which two words are antonyms?

○ A. Step and stride   ○ C. Learn and burn

○ B. Tall and short   ○ D. Boy and buoy

5TH GRADE • SOCIAL STUDIES

During which decade were "talkie" movies first made?

○ A. 1900s   ○ C. 1920s

○ B. 1910s   ○ D. 1930s

5TH GRADE • ENGLISH

Who wrote, "Bubble, bubble, toil and trouble"?

$1,000,000 Question

5TH GRADE • MUSIC

In classical music, who wrote *The Nutcracker*?

○ A. Wagner   ○ C. Chopin

○ B. Stravinsky   ○ D. Tchaikovsky

1ST GRADE • MEASUREMENTS

If you laid three rulers and two yardsticks end to end, how long would it be?

1ST GRADE • HISTORY

A boat that can travel completely beneath the water is called a _____.

2ND GRADE • HEALTH

Which does not help stop the spread of germs?

- ○ A. Covering your mouth when you cough
- ○ B. Sneezing into a tissue
- ○ C. Shaking hands
- ○ D. Antibiotics

2ND GRADE • VOCABULARY

Your distance above sea level is your _____.

3RD GRADE • MATH

Which is the ten thousands digit in 763,492?

3RD GRADE • EARTH SCIENCE

What gives green leaves their color?

4TH GRADE ▪ ASTRONOMY

What is the second largest planet in our solar system?

4TH GRADE ▪ U.S. HISTORY

What is the most common first name among U.S. presidents?

○ A. John ○ C. James

○ B. George ○ D. Millard

5TH GRADE ▪ WORLD HISTORY

Who was the leader of the Soviet Union during World War II?

5TH GRADE ▪ MATH

If y=3x, and 3x=36, then what number does "y" equal?

$1,000,000 Question

5TH GRADE ▪ MUSIC

What's another name for a tenor tuba?

○ A. French horn ○ C. Flugelhorn

○ B. Euphonium ○ D. Sousaphone

**Exceptional 5th Graders . . . Jean-Philippe
Baratier published articles in math by age 10.**

1ST GRADE • ENGLISH

What is the verb in the following sentence?
"The goat ran into the barn—boom!"

1ST GRADE • SOCIAL STUDIES

In U.S. currency, whose likeness is on the front of
the fifty-dollar bill?

2ND GRADE • WORLD GEOGRAPHY

❑ **True**   ❑ **False**

China is in the western hemisphere.

2ND GRADE • ANIMAL SCIENCE

❑ **True**   ❑ **False**

Penguins live almost exclusively in the arctic region
of the Earth.

3RD GRADE • MATH

Six football teams have 46 players each. How many
football players are there all together?

3RD GRADE • SPELLING

Spell the opposite of vertical.

4TH GRADE ▪ MEASUREMENTS

How many fluid ounces are in three pints?

4TH GRADE ▪ GEOGRAPHY

What is the tallest mountain in North America?

5TH GRADE ▪ U.S. HISTORY

Who was U.S. president when World War II ended?

5TH GRADE ▪ ASTRONOMY

Clusters of stars are known as _____.

$1,000,000 Question

5TH GRADE ▪ MATH

Which is the formula for area of a square, with A equaling area, and s equaling the length of one of the square's sides?

○ A. $A = 4s$

○ C. $A = perimeter \times pi$

○ B. $A = s \times s$

○ D. $A = s + s$

Why Wait Till Kindergarten? . . . Albert Wong began playing the violin at age 3. He won a grand prize in an 18-and-under competition when he was 5. By the time he was in 5th grade, he already had a CD on sale!

1ST GRADE ▪ SPELLING

Finish the following sentence: "I before E except after
_____."

1ST GRADE ▪ GEOGRAPHY

What direction do you have to travel to go from St.
Louis to Kansas City?

2ND GRADE ▪ GRAMMAR

What is the symbol between the parentheses
called? (&)

2ND GRADE ▪ MEASUREMENTS

In dry weight, how many ounces are in a pound?

3RD GRADE ▪ SOCIAL STUDIES

Which of the following inventions was NOT invented
in China?

◯ A. Gunpowder   ◯ C. Kites

◯ B. Cultured pearls   ◯ D. Paper

3RD GRADE ▪ MUSIC

Which of the following is not a keyboard instrument?

○ A. Theremin   ○ C. Harmonium

○ B. Clavichord   ○ D. Harpsichord

4TH GRADE ▪ MATH

In square inches, what is the surface area of a cube with five-inch sides?

4TH GRADE ▪ GEOGRAPHY

What is the capital of New Mexico?

5TH GRADE ▪ MATH

Which is true of a 40-degree angle?

○ A. It is straight.   ○ C. It is right.

○ B. It is obtuse.   ○ D. It is acute.

5TH GRADE ▪ U.S. HISTORY

What event took the world to the brink of World War III in 1962?

○ A. Building of the Berlin Wall

○ B. Cuban Missile Crisis

○ C. Assassination of President Kennedy

○ D. Start of the Vietnam War

$1,000,000 Question

5TH GRADE ▪ HISTORY

Where was the first atom bomb detonated?

1st Grade ▪ U.S. History

How many stripes (both red and white) are there on the U.S flag?

1st Grade ▪ Animal Science

Land animals breathe with lungs. Fish breathe with _____.

2nd Grade ▪ Grammar

How many plural nouns are in the following sentence? "Over the barn, geese flew between the raindrops."

2nd Grade ▪ Spelling

Spell the word that goes in the blank. "Shhhhhh! Please be _____."

3rd Grade ▪ World Geography

❑ **True**   ❑ **False**

The equator goes through Australia.

3rd Grade ▪ Human Science

Which term best describes the human heart?

○ A. Bone   ○ C. Ligament

○ B. Muscle   ○ D. Cartilage

4TH GRADE ▪ U.S. GEOGRAPHY

Name the five Great Lakes.

4TH GRADE ▪ U.S. GEOGRAPHY

What is the capital of Alabama?

5TH GRADE ▪ CHEMISTRY

What element is the fourth most abundant in the universe, and also contained in every living thing on Earth?

5TH GRADE ▪ COMPUTER

In the names of many web sites, what does the "www" stand for?

$1,000,000 Question

5TH GRADE ▪ ANIMAL SCIENCE

What is the largest fish in the world?

5th Grade Heroes . . . 11-year-old Kyle Slyman, from Burnaby, British Columbia, in Canada, became a hero when his class went on a field trip to a local pool. When Kyle saw a classmate lying at the bottom of the pool Kyle swam to the bottom, put an arm around the boy's torso, and pulled him to the surface. The boy recovered completely thanks to Kyle's quick thinking.

QUIZ NUMBER 69

1ST GRADE ▪ READING

Who wrote *The Cat in the Hat*?

1ST GRADE ▪ ART

To keep your clothes clean while painting, it's best to wear a _____.

2ND GRADE ▪ ANIMAL SCIENCE

A turtle is a _____.

○ A. Fish   ○ C. Amphibian

○ B. Reptile   ○ D. Mammal

2ND GRADE ▪ SOCIAL STUDIES

In which city is the headquarters for the United Nations?

3RD GRADE ▪ U.S. HISTORY

What general lost the Battle of the Little Big Horn?

3RD GRADE ▪ SCIENCE

What is the lowest layer of the Earth's atmosphere?

○ A. Mesosphere   ○ C. Troposphere

○ B. Thermosphere ○ D. Unisphere

4TH GRADE • MATH

In the equation eight divided by four equals two, which number represents the dividend?

4TH GRADE • WORLD GEOGRAPHY

In land area, what is the second largest continent?

5TH GRADE • SCIENCE

At sea level, water begins to boil at how many degrees Fahrenheit?

5TH GRADE • WORLD GEOGRAPHY

What is the tallest mountain in South America?

- ○ A. Mt. Aconcagua
- ○ B. Mt. Chimborazo
- ○ C. Mt. Huascaran
- ○ D. Mt. Pico Bolivar

$1,000,000 Question

5TH GRADE • BIOLOGY

What is the largest artery in the human body?

**No He Di-N't. Yes He Di-Id.
Geometry wiz Blaise Pascal, at
age 10, worked out the first 23
"Propositions of Euclid" on his own.**

1ST GRADE ▪ ART

Which of the following is not a secondary color?

- ○ A. Orange
- ○ B. Red
- ○ C. Green
- ○ D. Purple

1ST GRADE ▪ MATH

If it takes Dave three days to walk to the other side of the forest, but a day less to get back, how many days did it take Dave to make the round trip?

2ND GRADE ▪ MEASUREMENTS

What's longer, a kilometer or a mile?

2ND GRADE ▪ HISTORY

❑ **True**   ❑ **False**

The sixteenth century is also known as the 1500s.

3RD GRADE ▪ ASTRONOMY

On which planet would a person weigh the most?

- ○ A. Mercury
- ○ B. Saturn
- ○ C. Jupiter
- ○ D. Earth

3RD GRADE ▪ WORLD GEOGRAPHY

Not counting Australia, what is the largest island on Earth?

4TH GRADE • MATH

Between 1 and 100, how many multiples of 9 are odd numbers?

4TH GRADE • ENGLISH

How many articles are in the following sentence? "I went to the fruit stand and bought a banana and an apple."

5TH GRADE • U.S. GEOGRAPHY

What two U.S. states border Washington, D.C.?

5TH GRADE • WORLD GEOGRAPHY

What is the world's second largest country in terms of land area?

$1,000,000 Question

5TH GRADE • ALGEBRA

If $32y = 64x$, what does y equal?

Didja Know? . . . Anna Paquin won the Best Supporting Actress Oscar at age 11 for her role in the move *The Piano*. Today she is best known as Rogue in the *X-Men* movies.

1ST GRADE ▪ HISTORY

Which country never fought in a war against the United States?

○ A. England   ○ C. Spain

○ B. Italy   ○ D. Brazil

1ST GRADE ▪ MEASUREMENTS

How many months in the year have 31 days?

2ND GRADE ▪ MATH

How many hours are there in three days?

2ND GRADE ▪ ANIMAL SCIENCE

A giant panda's natural habitat is on what continent?

3RD GRADE ▪ MATH

How many of the interior angles in a scalene triangle have the same number of degrees?

3RD GRADE ▪ GEOGRAPHY

The Tropic of Cancer is in which hemisphere?

4TH GRADE ▪ ASTRONOMY

Other than Earth, name the five planets that can be seen with the naked eye.

4TH GRADE ▪ CHEMISTRY

On the periodic table, which element is represented by the letters "Kr"?

5TH GRADE ▪ U.S. HISTORY

In what year was the U.S. Constitution written?

5TH GRADE ▪ SOCIAL STUDIES

What is the official currency of Puerto Rico?

$1,000,000 Question

5TH GRADE ▪ MATH

What is $^6/_6$, expressed as a decimal?

> **Because It's There . . . In 2006 5th grader Jordan Romero became the youngest person ever to climb the summit of Mount Kilimanjaro in Africa. It took him three days to get to the top. His advice to other 5th graders: "Always follow your dreams."**

1st Grade ▪ Geography

What is the only continent that is also a country?

1st Grade ▪ Art

What two colors do you blend together to make orange?

2nd Grade ▪ Social Studies

The Inca civilization was based on what continent?

2nd Grade ▪ Life Science

❏ **True**   ❏ **False**

A hummingbird can fly backward.

3rd Grade ▪ Math

Lisa, Rita and Patty equally share 1,242 gumballs. How many does each girl get?

3rd Grade ▪ Human Science

❏ **True**   ❏ **False**

The bones at the base of your spine are known as the lumbar vertebrae.

4TH GRADE ▪ MEASUREMENTS

How many days were there in the year 1980?

4TH GRADE ▪ SOCIAL STUDIES

According to the Constitution, how many years must you have lived in the United States in order to become president?

5TH GRADE ▪ WORLD GEOGRAPHY

The Mediterranean Island of Corsica is part of what European country?

5TH GRADE ▪ PHYSICAL SCIENCE

Density describes the mass of an object divided by the what?

$1,000,000 Question

5TH GRADE ▪ ENGLISH

Assigning human characteristics to non-human entities is called _____.

○ A. Allegory   ○ C. Anthropomorphism

○ B. Simile   ○ D. Neo-romantic

Oldest American School . . . The oldest public school in America is the Boston Latin School in Boston, Massachusetts, which first opened its doors for learning on April 23, 1635.

QUIZ NUMBER 73

1ST GRADE ▪ ANIMAL SCIENCE

❏ **True**   ❏ **False**

A bottlenose dolphin is a fish.

1ST GRADE ▪ SOCIAL STUDIES

In U.S. currency, whose image appears on the front of the $20 bill?

2ND GRADE ▪ ANIMAL SCIENCE

❏ **True**   ❏ **False**

The opossum is a marsupial.

2ND GRADE ▪ ART

What two colors when mixed together make purple?

3RD GRADE ▪ GEOLOGY

❏ **True**   ❏ **False**

Marble is a metamorphic rock.

3RD GRADE ▪ HISTORY

How many decades are in a millennium?

Between 1 and 100, how many multiples of 5 are odd numbers?

How many right angles are there in a right triangle?

- ○ A. None
- ○ B. One
- ○ C. Two
- ○ D. Three

In the world of music, which of the following is a reed instrument?

- ○ A. French horn
- ○ B. Recorder
- ○ C. Flute
- ○ D. Clarinet

Which of the following is not the name of a Native American tribe?

- ○ A. Kwakiutl
- ○ B. Inuit
- ○ C. Tecumseh
- ○ D. Assiniboine

$1,000,000 Question

What is the softest rock?

Reaching for the Stars . . . At age 10, Truman Henry Safford could square 18-digit numbers in his head. As an adult he became an astronomer.

1ST GRADE ▪ ARITHMETIC

If you added up all of the numerals 1 through 9, what is the sum?

1ST GRADE ▪ GEOGRAPHY

Florida borders Georgia and what other U.S. state?

2ND GRADE ▪ SOCIAL STUDIES

What is the official language of Mexico?

2ND GRADE ▪ ASTRONOMY

How many moons does the planet Mars have?

3RD GRADE ▪ GEOMETRY

What is the least number of corners that a polygon can have?

3RD GRADE ▪ MATH

If there are 12 slices of pie and Henry eats 6 of them, which fraction represents the portion of the pie Henry ate?

○ A. $\frac{3}{8}$ ○ C. $\frac{3}{5}$

○ B. $\frac{1}{2}$ ○ D. $\frac{7}{10}$

4TH GRADE ▪ ART

Which artist painted *Self-Portrait With Bandaged Ear and Pipe?*

4TH GRADE ▪ ENGLISH

What is the adverb in the following sentence? "The waitress moved briskly through the crowded restaurant."

5TH GRADE ▪ WORLD HISTORY

According to Greek mythology, who was the ruler of all the gods?

5TH GRADE ▪ SOCIAL STUDIES

What is the Canadian Shield?

- ○ A. A plateau in Canada
- ○ B. The maple leaf on the Canadian flag
- ○ C. A unit in the Canadian army
- ○ D. Canada's coat of arms

$1,000,000 Question

5TH GRADE ▪ MATH

With the fractions $5/7$ and $7/10$, what is the lowest common denominator?

- ○ A. 17
- ○ C. 3
- ○ B. 70
- ○ D. 29

> King of the Cyberheads . . . While in fifth grade, Steve Wozniak began developing complex electronics. He went on to develop the world's first screen and keyboard desktop computer.

1st Grade ▪ Arithmetic

What is the difference between 111 and 64?

1st Grade ▪ Grammar

In the following sentence, which word is the pronoun? "Mommy gave him lunch money today."

2nd Grade ▪ English

What is the plural form for the word "moose"?

2nd Grade ▪ Science

Using the Fahrenheit scale, at what temperature does water freeze?

3rd Grade ▪ Earth Science

Entomologists primarily study what?

- ○ A. Volcanoes
- ○ B. Energy sources
- ○ C. Insects
- ○ D. Weather

3rd Grade ▪ U.S. Geography

Which is the capital of Nebraska?

- ○ A. Boise
- ○ B. Lincoln
- ○ C. Little Rock
- ○ D. Omaha

What is the square root of 64?

○ A. 8

○ C. 9

○ B. 7

○ D. $6\frac{1}{2}$

Who assassinated Abraham Lincoln?

○ A. Lee Harvey Oswald

○ C. John Wilkes Booth

○ B. Mark David Chapman

○ D. Sirhan Sirhan

Express the fraction $\frac{9}{20}$ as a decimal.

○ A. .920

○ C. .40

○ B. .45

○ D. 2.2

Where was the first European settlement in what is now the United States?

○ A. Jamestown, Virginia

○ C. St. Augustine, Florida

○ B. Plymouth, Massachusetts

○ D. Roanoke, Virginia

★ $1,000,000 Question

Which part of your brain controls your sight?

5th Grade Phenom . . . By the time he was 10 years old, musician Yo Yo Ma was already a master cellist.

Quiz 1

1st Grade Social Studies	October.
1st Grade World Geography	False. Africa is a continent made up of many countries. It is south of Europe, though.
2nd Grade U.S. Geography	The Gulf of Mexico.
2nd Grade English	Four: Mis-sis-sip-pi.
3rd Grade World History	False. The year 1492 was near the end of the fifteenth century.
3rd Grade Measurements	There are 225 feet in 75 yards, three feet to a yard.
4th Grade Earth Science	False. Comets are comprised mostly of ice and dust.
4th Grade Chemistry	Nitrogen.
5th Grade Math	Less.
5th Grade Biology	A. The frontal lobe of your brain controls your learning and decision making.
$1,000,000	The instruments that most normally comprise a string quartet are: two violins, a viola and a cello.

Quiz 2

1st Grade U.S. History	Bill Clinton.
1st Grade English	The word "ran" is the verb.
2nd Grade Measurements	There are 72 inches in two yards.
2nd Grade Government	Albany is the capital of New York.
3rd Grade Earth Science	A. The Missouri is 2,540 miles long. The Mississippi is 2,340, the Rio Grande is 1,900 miles, and the Ohio is 1,290 miles.

3rd Grade Human Science	The thigh bone is known to doctors as the femur.
4th Grade Math	The yard is 1,000 square feet in size.
4th Grade Chemistry	D. Carbon dioxide is not a noble gas. A noble gas—such as helium, neon, and argon—can conduct electricity and be made to create its own light (fluoresce).
5th Grade U.S. History	B. Hancock's famous signature was on the Declaration of Independence, not on the Constitution.
5th Grade Chemistry	A. Salt is made up of sodium and chlorine. The chemical formula for salt is written NaCl.
$1,000,000	According to *National Geographic Explorer!*, the tuatara has a third eye on top of its head. Although it does not "see" as in offer vision, scientists believe the organ may be used to tell time or determine the season.

QUIZ 3

1st Grade Art	Pink comes from mixing red with white.
1st Grade Science	The three states of matter are solid, liquid and gas.
2nd Grade English	In the word "unnecessary," the "un" is the prefix.
2nd Grade Grammar	The plural of the word "deer" is deer.
3rd Grade Geography	The Pacific Ocean.
3rd Grade U.S. History	C. The sinking of the *Arizona* occurred during the Japanese attack at Pearl Harbor, Hawaii, on December 7, 1941.
4th Grade Math	7.
4th Grade Human Science	B. Pituitary gland.
5th Grade Math	The lowest common denominator for 3/4 and 4/7 is 28.
5th Grade U.S. History	Alan Shepherd. His sub-orbital flight took place on May 5, 1961.
$1,000,000	An octahedron is a solid (three-dimensional) figure with eight faces.

1st Grade Science	Oxygen.
1st Grade U.S. Geography	Maine shares a border with New Hampshire.
2nd Grade Math	D. $14 \times 5 = 70$.
2nd Grade World Geography	Canada.
3rd Grade Music	D. Drums are a percussion instrument.
3rd Grade U.S. History	The northernmost Civil War battle took place in and around Gettysburg, Pennsylvania during July 1863.
4th Grade U.S. History	B. Passed in 1764 by England, the new tax helped start the movement for independence that led to the American Revolution.
4th Grade Math	Each will have 714 baseball cards.
5th Grade Art	C. Leonardo da Vinci painted the *Mona Lisa* in 1503.
5th Grade Geography	False.
$1,000,000	General William Westmoreland led U.S. forces in Vietnam.

Quiz 5

1st Grade Science	False. A whale is not a fish at all. It is a mammal.
1st Grade History	Thomas Edison invented the lightbulb.
2nd Grade Math	C. 7 goes into 49 seven times.
2nd Grade Spelling	"Witch" should be spelled "Which" when used in this context.
3rd Grade Science	A paleontologist studies ancient life, such as the dinosaurs.
3rd Grade Geography	The Tropic of Capricorn is in the southern hemisphere.
4th Grade Punctuation	B. The word "it's" only has an apostrophe when it is a contraction. It is written "its" when it indicates the possessive.
4th Grade U.S. History	B. The Mason-Dixon line was created in 1763 to mark the boundary between

the property of the Penn family and the Calvert family. The line later became associated with slavery.

5th Grade Astronomy	Asteroids.
5th Grade Science	D. Sunshine is necessary for photosynthesis to occur.
$1,000,000	The smallest fish in the world is the dwarf pygmy Gobi. They hardly ever grow to be more than one-half inch long.

QUIZ 6

1st Grade Measurements	There are 12 inches in a foot.
1st Grade Social Studies	Abraham Lincoln.
2nd Grade Astronomy	Saturn.
2nd Grade Math	There are 6 zeroes in 1,000,000 (one million).
3rd Grade Geography	B. The Nile River in Africa is 4,132 miles long.
3rd Grade Math	D. $3/4 + 1/2$ (or $2/4$) = $5/4$ (or $1\ 1/4$).
4th Grade Earth Science	Diamond.
4th Grade U.S. History	The allies invaded at the beaches of Normandy, France.
5th Grade Math	8. The square root of 65 is about 8.06.
5th Grade Science	C. The water that comes out the bottom is the amount not absorbed.
$1,000,000	1.31 meters.

QUIZ 7

1st Grade English	One. "Rude" is the only adjective in this sentence.
1st Grade Animal Science	True. A lizard is a reptile.
2nd Grade Animal Science	True. The kangaroo is a marsupial.
2nd Grade World History	Africa.
3rd Grade Geometry	A quadrangle has four sides.
3rd Grade World Geography	Australia is known as the "Island Continent."
4th Grade U.S. History	False. John Adams (the second president) was the father of John Quincy Adams (the sixth president).

4th Grade World Geography	B. The easternmost country in Africa is Somalia.
5th Grade Science	D. Membrane.
5th Grade History	A. The telegraph was invented first, in 1837. The motorized vacuum cleaner was invented in 1899. The neon lamp made its debut in 1910. And the Wright Brothers first flew at Kitty Hawk in 1903.
$1,000,000	M-A-S-S-A-C-H-U-S-E-T-T-S.

Quiz 8

1st Grade Math	There are 60 seconds in a minute.
1st Grade English	The word "chair" is the noun.
2nd Grade Spelling	Alabama.
2nd Grade Animal Science	The kangaroo's natural habitat is Australia.
3rd Grade Math	Never. Parallel lines do not intersect.
3rd Grade Earth Science	Igneous rock comes out of volcanoes, in the form of molten magma.
4th Grade Measurements	There are 32 ounces in a quart.
4th Grade World Geography	C. The Panama Canal connects the Atlantic and Pacific Oceans.
5th Grade Math	The answer is 4 with a remainder of 1.
5th Grade Science	Carbon dioxide is not a product of photosynthesis.
$1,000,000	Four.

Quiz 9

1st Grade Grammar	Two. "Bill" and "Oklahoma" are proper nouns.
1st Grade Measurements	Four. April, June, September and November have only 30 days.
2nd Grade U.S. History	Mount Rushmore.
2nd Grade U.S. Geography	D. Los Angeles has the second-largest population. Chicago for many years was the second-largest city in the country, but L.A. passed it in size during the late 20th century.

3rd Grade Math	You correctly say the number 4.07 as "four and seven hundredths."
3rd Grade Science	The exosphere.
4th Grade U.S. History	The axis powers of World War II were Japan, Germany and Italy.
4th Grade Music	B. The brass section.
5th Grade Social Studies	C. They dyed their shoes.
5th Grade English	Shakespeare put those words in *Hamlet*.
$1,000,000	There are 180 degrees in a straight angle.

Quiz 10

1st Grade English	Five. The consonants in baseball are b, s, b, l and l.
1st Grade Measurements	There are 365 days in the year. Leap years have one more day (February 29).
2nd Grade Math	There are 40 nickels in 2 dollars.
2nd Grade Spelling	The word is spelled B-E-A-U-T-I-F-U-L.
3rd Grade Math	True.
3rd Grade Science	False. A chameleon can turn pink.
4th Grade Science	A light-year is the distance light travels in one year.
4th Grade Earth Science	June.
5th Grade World History	D. They are all explorers.
5th Grade U.S. Geography	The four states are Utah, Colorado, Arizona and New Mexico.
$1,000,000	B. One hundred pounds.

Quiz 11

1st Grade Math	Fourteen cents.
1st Grade Science	True. All mammals are warm-blooded.
2nd Grade Social Studies	False. Hispanics can come from any Spanish-speaking nation.
2nd Grade Grammar	C. The preferred plural of octopus is "octopi."
3rd Grade Math	The answer to a subtraction problem is the difference.
3rd Grade Health	B. The chicken is a consumer in a food chain.

4th Grade Astronomy	The Great Bear (or The Big Bear).
4th Grade Chemistry	Carbon.
5th Grade History	B. 1614.
5th Grade Earth Science	C. Seismic.
$1,000,000	The "Ode to Joy" comes from Beethoven's ninth and last symphony.

QUIZ 12

1st Grade Math	Seventeen minutes.
1st Grade Music	A typical guitar has six strings.
2nd Grade English	The word "blue" is the adjective.
2nd Grade Phys. Ed.	D. There is no head turning while doing jumping jacks.
3rd Grade English	One. The word "loudly" is an adverb. ("Portly" is an adjective.)
3rd Grade Human Science	False. The smallest bone in the human body is the stirrup bone, and it's inside your ear.
4th Grade Physics	C. Inertia, also known as "Newton's 1st Law of Motion."
4th Grade U.S. History	Franklin Delano Roosevelt.
5th Grade Science	SOund Navigation And Ranging.
5th Grade Ancient History	B. 4th century B.C.
$1,000,000	M-O-C-C-A-S-I-N-S.

QUIZ 13

1st Grade English	Little Boy Blue.
1st Grade Math	Five touchdowns and five extra points would need to be scored. (6 + 1 = 7, 7 × 5 = 35.)
2nd Grade English	In the word "directly," the "ly" is the suffix.
2nd Grade Dance	Ballet dancers sometimes dance on their toes.
3rd Grade U.S. History	John Glenn. He orbited the Earth three times on February 20, 1962.
3rd Grade Biology	A. The left side of the heart pumps blood outward to most of the human body.

4th Grade World Geography	The Alps.
4th Grade U.S. History	B. Utah.
5th Grade History	B. 1607.
5th Grade Literature	L. Frank Baum.
$1,000,000	France and Spain.

QUIZ 14

1st Grade Measurements	There are 100 years in a century.
1st Grade U.S. Geography	California shares a border with Oregon, Nevada and Arizona. It also shares a border with the country of Mexico.
2nd Grade Animal Science	Among birds, the ostrich lays the largest eggs.
2nd Grade Music	C. The conductor does not write the music. The music is written by the composer.
3rd Grade Art	Michelangelo painted the ceiling of the Sistine Chapel, with scenes from the Bible, from 1511–1512.
3rd Grade Math	9 × 39 = 351, which is less than 360.
4th Grade Health	D. Bacteria.
4th Grade Math	The field is 4,500 square yards in size.
5th Grade U.S. Geography	Arizona and Nevada.
5th Grade U.S. History	The Republican Party.
$1,000,000	B. Counting tree rings.

QUIZ 15

1st Grade Art	D. Green is a secondary color comprised of blue and yellow.
1st Grade Animal Science	True. Turtles are cold-blooded.
2nd Grade World Geography	Canada is on North America.
2nd Grade Grammar	Two. "Billy" and "Ballpark" are singular nouns.
3rd Grade Spelling	The holiday is spelled L-A-B-O-R D-A-Y.
3rd Grade Math	n = 9.
4th Grade Music	A. Germany.
4th Grade Geography	Mount Kilimanjaro (19, 340 feet) is the tallest mountain in Africa.

5th Grade Astronomy	Shooting stars are actually meteorites.
5th Grade U.S. History	C. Jimmy Carter.
$1,000,000	The world's longest insect is the Stick Insect, which can grow to be as long as 22 inches.

Quiz 16

1st Grade English	"My mother" is the subject of the sentence.
1st Grade Social Studies	Thomas Jefferson's likeness is on the nickel.
2nd Grade Math	399.
2nd Grade Measurements	There are 100 centimeters in a meter.
3rd Grade Biology	False. We have no "medium intestine."
3rd Grade Maps	A. Topography, or land forms.
4th Grade Animal Science	B. Africa.
4th Grade World Geography	C. West Indies.
5th Grade World History	C. Balboa. He crossed at the Isthmus of Panama.
5th Grade U.S. History	B. Ireland.
$1,000,000	The numbers are 2, 3, 5 and 7.

Quiz 17

1st Grade Music	D. The tuba is not a woodwind instrument.
1st Grade Spelling	The test is multiple C-H-O-I-C-E.
2nd Grade English	The word "quickly" is the adverb.
2nd Grade Measurements	You need 5 coins (half dollar, dime, three pennies).
3rd Grade Math	A pentagon has 5 sides.
3rd Grade Biology	B. The liver is part of the digestive system.
4th Grade Geography	The westernmost country in Africa is Senegal.
4th Grade Phys. Ed.	45 feet.
5th Grade Health	C. Bean.
5th Grade Biology	Nucleus.
$1,000,000	A. Windshield wipers were invented in 1903. Cornflakes were invented in

1906, color photography in 1907, and cellophane in 1908.

Quiz 18

1st Grade Measurements	10 feet.
1st Grade Animal Science	A human being is a mammal.
2nd Grade English	The letter "e" is silent.
2nd Grade Animal Science	D. African elephants have much larger ears than their Asian counterparts.
3rd Grade Math	False. All sides are the same length in an equilateral triangle.
3rd Grade U.S. History	West Virginia was formed because of the Civil War when people in the western part of the state did not want to secede from the union.
4th Grade World Geography	C. South America.
4th Grade Science	Plants.
5th Grade Earth Science	C. Weathering.
5th Grade Phys. Ed.	C. The Marquess of Queensbury.
$1,000,000	1920s.

Quiz 19

1st Grade Grammar	Three. Pennsylvania, Petula and Popcorn are all proper nouns.
1st Grade Social Studies	Braille.
2nd Grade Spelling	Wyoming.
2nd Grade History	False. The 17th century is also known as the 1600s.
3rd Grade Science	Jets usually fly in the stratosphere.
3rd Grade Math	There are 130 ballplayers in total.
4th Grade U.S. History	C. The Spanish-American War was fought predominantly in Cuba.
4th Grade Biology	A. Ligaments.
5th Grade English	Harriet Beecher Stowe.
5th Grade Spelling	C-A-R-I-B-B-E-A-N.
$1,000,000	C. $1/1,000,000$ of a meter.

1st Grade English	They are vowels.
1st Grade Health	D. The carrot has no seeds.
2nd Grade Science	Glaciers.
2nd Grade English	Ann is third.
3rd Grade Social Studies	True.
3rd Grade Math	5. $\frac{5}{9}$ is greater than $\frac{1}{2}$.
4th Grade U.S. History	They are George Washington, Thomas Jefferson, Theodore Roosevelt and Abraham Lincoln.
4th Grade Art	Michelangelo carved the statue of David.
5th Grade U.S. History	Jefferson Davis was the president of the Confederate States of America.
5th Grade Social Studies	The letters stand for Federal Bureau of Investigation.
$1,000,000	D. The ocean is an aquatic biome, not a terrestrial biome.

QUIZ 21

1st Grade History	The telephone.
1st Grade U.S. Geography	False. Georgia borders on the Atlantic Ocean, not the Gulf of Mexico.
2nd Grade Math	The answer to a multiplication problem is called the product.
2nd Grade Dance	A. Square Dance.
3rd Grade Vocabulary	To dilute is to make weaker.
3rd Grade U.S. History	B. The Emancipation Proclamation, signed by President Abraham Lincoln.
4th Grade Astronomy	The nearest star to the Earth is the Sun.
4th Grade Chemistry	Oxygen.
5th Grade Math	The integers are 30 and 29.
5th Grade World Geography	Africa.
$1,000,000	The 18th century. The first bicycles were called "dandy-horses."

QUIZ 22

1st Grade Phys. Ed.	The goalie.
1st Grade U.S. History	D. The Declaration of Independence.

2nd Grade English	Forget.
2nd Grade World Geography	South America.
3rd Grade Spelling	V-E-R-T-I-C-A-L.
3rd Grade Human Science	False. The knuckles are saddle and hinge joints, not ball-and-socket.
4th Grade Math	The dance floor is 300 square feet in size.
4th Grade Social Studies	C. Massachusetts.
5th Grade Phys. Ed.	Skateboarding.
5th Grade Biology	C. Chloroplast is found in a plant cell only.
$1,000,000	Lewis Carroll.

Quiz 23

1st Grade Math	15.
1st Grade U.S. History	Thomas Jefferson was the third U.S. president.
2nd Grade Music	C. Jazz.
2nd Grade Animal Science	D. Africa.
3rd Grade Grammar	"Baseball" is the compound word.
3rd Grade Chemistry	B. Compound.
4th Grade Geography	Mount Blanc (15,771 feet) is the tallest mountain in Europe.
4th Grade U.S. History	Edwin E. "Buzz" Aldrin. He stepped onto the Moon seconds after the first man, Neil Armstrong.
5th Grade Science	Cumulonimbus.
5th Grade English	D. Delicate.
$1,000,000	H-U-C-K-L-E-B-E-R-R-Y.

Quiz 24

1st Grade English	Little Jack Horner committed that act.
1st Grade U.S. Geography	None. The state of Hawaii is comprised of a series of islands in the Pacific Ocean.
2nd Grade Maps	Six inches.
2nd Grade Science	A. Prism.
3rd Grade Measurements	0 degrees Celsius is warmer. It is equivalent to 32 degrees Fahrenheit.
3rd Grade Spelling	C-L-E-O-P-A-T-R-A.

4th Grade U.S. Geography	C. Alabama is known as The Cotton State.
4th Grade U.S. History	Grover Cleveland.
5th Grade English	14.
5th Grade Earth Science	C. Metamorphic.
$1,000,000	A. 800 B.C.

QUIZ 25

1st Grade Spelling & Grammar	T-E-E-T-H.
1st Grade Science	C. Every magnet is surrounded by a magnetic field.
2nd Grade Social Studies	Members of Congress.
2nd Grade Astronomy	Pegasus.
3rd Grade Math	3.74.
3rd Grade Geography	B. Istanbul.
4th Grade Spelling	M-A-S-C-A-R-A.
4th Grade Grammar	A. Blue and blew. Homonyms are words that are pronounced the same but spelled differently.
5th Grade Astronomy	Orbits that are not round are called elliptical.
5th Grade Computer	Central Processing Unit.
$1,000,000	B. The concertina resembles a small accordion.

QUIZ 26

1st Grade English	A comma should go between the words "pears" and "apples."
1st Grade Social Studies	A picture of the Lincoln Memorial is on the back of the penny.
2nd Grade Science	One day. The Earth rotates once every 24 hours.
2nd Grade Measurements	There are 1,000 meters in a kilometer.
3rd Grade World Geography	C. Canberra is the capital of Australia.
3rd Grade U.S. History	C. The Bill of Rights guarantees personal freedoms.
4th Grade Geometry	A heptagon has seven sides.
4th Grade Grammar	A. Step and stride.
5th Grade Science	D. Astronomy.

5th Grade Computer	Random Access Memory.
$1,000,000	The *Endeavour*.

1st Grade Spelling	The response to a question is the A-N-S-W-E-R.
1st Grade U.S. Geography	The Statue of Liberty stands in New York Harbor.
2nd Grade Measurements	There are 3 gallons in 12 quarts (4 quarts to a gallon).
2nd Grade U.S. History	C. The president runs the executive branch of the U.S. government.
3rd Grade Math	An octagon has eight sides.
3rd Grade Science	D. The bubbles are made of carbon dioxide.
4th Grade Geography	The northernmost country in Africa is Tunisia.
4th Grade World History	Sir Edmund Hillary.
5th Grade Literature	Mark Twain.
5th Grade Ocean Science	A black smoker.
$1,000,000	Instant coffee was the first of these inventions (instant coffee, 1909; the Band-Aid, 1920; the modern zipper, 1913; stainless steel, 1916).

1st Grade Phys. Ed.	It's called a double play.
1st Grade Animal Science	True. A mouse is a mammal.
2nd Grade U.S. Geography	St. Louis, Missouri, features the "Gateway to the West."
2nd Grade Animal Science	False. The Green Iguana eats mostly plants.
3rd Grade Math	An isosceles triangle has two sides (and two angles) that are equal in length.
3rd Grade Health	B. Louis Pasteur.
4th Grade Literature	V-O-L-D-E-M-O-R-T.
4th Grade U.S. History	Benjamin Franklin.
5th Grade Health	Fats.

5th Grade Computer	B. 1946—although it didn't begin computing until the following year.
$1,000,000	B. 40.

1st Grade Grammar	The word "can't" is a contraction.
1st Grade Math	False. $3 \times 4 = 12$. $3 \times 3 \times 3 \times 3 = 81$.
2nd Grade Measurements	B. 1.7 centimeters.
2nd Grade World Geography	Atlantic Ocean.
3rd Grade Animal Science	B. South America.
3rd Grade Literature & Spelling	H-E-R-M-I-O-N-E.
4th Grade U.S. History	Richard Nixon resigned on August 9, 1974, because of his involvement in the Watergate scandal.
4th Grade Art	B. Cubist.
5th Grade Astronomy	Yuri Gagarin.
5th Grade World History	18th century.
$1,000,000	Abraham Lincoln, James Garfield, William McKinley and John F. Kennedy.

Quiz 30

1st Grade Literature	She flies by tornado.
1st Grade U.S. History	The Civil War.
2nd Grade Astronomy	The Milky Way.
2nd Grade Phys. Ed.	B. Dodgeball and kickball use the same ball.
3rd Grade Math	$7/8 - 3/4$ (or $6/8$) $= 1/8$.
3rd Grade Phys. Ed.	B. Pull-ups and chin-ups are virtually the same thing except for the grip.
4th Grade Geography	Hawaii is the southernmost U.S. state.
4th Grade World History	Mahatma Gandhi.
5th Grade Geometry	C. Obtuse.
5th Grade Astronomy	B. 1564.
$1,000,000	Michael Faraday.

Quiz 31

1st Grade Science	D. The herbivore won't eat steak—or any other kind of meat.
1st Grade Earth Science	Sand is melted to make glass.

2nd Grade Math	20 percent.
2nd Grade U.S. History	The president's name was Millard Fill-more.
3rd Grade World History	Asia.
3rd Grade U.S. Geography	The Colorado River.
4th Grade Astronomy	Venus.
4th Grade Chemistry	Boron.
5th Grade Dance	B. Waltz.
5th Grade Literature	D. Harper Lee.
$1,000,000	Enrico Fermi.

QUIZ 32

1st Grade Phys. Ed.	D. Basketball.
1st Grade Animal Science	The giraffe is the world's tallest animal, winner by a neck.
2nd Grade English	3. Mary, Bill and Kansas.
2nd Grade World Geography	Kenya is on Africa.
3rd Grade Physics	C. Wavelength changes a sound's pitch.
3rd Grade Human Science	True. The shoulder is a ball-and-socket joint.
4th Grade World History	Berlin.
4th Grade Earth Science	September.
5th Grade English	A. Moonbeam.
5th Grade Literature	D. Ernest Hemingway.
$1,000,000	A. 3y = x.

QUIZ 33

1st Grade English	A limerick is a short and often funny poem.
1st Grade Animal Science	C. Insects.
2nd Grade Math	9.
2nd Grade U.S. History	The president's name was Chester Arthur.
3rd Grade Phys. Ed.	True.
3rd Grade World History	Marco Polo.
4th Grade Social Studies	B. Popular.
4th Grade Health	Your eyes move quickly. REM stands for Rapid Eye Movement.

5th Grade Spelling	A. Infrared.
5th Grade Art	C. Gauguin.
$1,000,000	The world's deadliest snake is the Black Mamba. One bite releases enough venom to kill 200 people.

Quiz 34

1st Grade Phys. Ed.	B. The long jump and the broad jump are the same thing.
1st Grade U.S. Geography	Alaska is the northernmost U.S. state.
2nd Grade Math	12.
2nd Grade English	2. They are "am" and "do."
3rd Grade Earth Science	On the Earth's surface. Air pressure decreases with altitude.
3rd Grade Geometry	False. The sum of the lengths of the sides of a figure is its perimeter.
4th Grade Social Studies	True.
4th Grade U.S. History	A golden spike was driven.
5th Grade World Geography	The Atlantic Ocean.
5th Grade Health	Insulin.
$1,000,000	William Howard Taft started the "7th inning stretch" on April 14, 1910.

Quiz 35

1st Grade English	Jack jumped over the candlestick.
1st Grade Phys. Ed.	Crunches exercise the stomach region (abdominal muscles, abs).
2nd Grade U.S. Geography	The Mississippi River runs through New Orleans, Louisiana.
2nd Grade Astronomy	The Earth takes one year to go completely around the Sun.
3rd Grade Vocabulary	Stronger.
3rd Grade Biology	C. The heart is in the circulatory system.
4th Grade Grammar	Two articles: "The" and "the."
4th Grade World History	The Soviet Union's government was Communist.
5th Grade Astronomy	None. Venus has no moons.

5th Grade Music	B. The clarinet is largest of those instruments.
$1,000,000	Dalí's paintings are surrealist.

1st Grade English	One. The word "beautiful" is the only adjective.
1st Grade Social Studies	"Two bits" is the same as 25 cents, or a quarter.
2nd Grade World History	Europe.
2nd Grade Measurements	There are 1,000 grams in a kilogram.
3rd Grade Math	27,000.
3rd Grade Animal Science	A kingdom is the grouping that has the most animals in it.
4th Grade Earth Science	C. Tuber.
4th Grade U.S. History	B. Rich port.
5th Grade Physical Science	D. Pulley.
5th Grade World Geography	The Pyranees.
$1,000,000	D. Minnesota.

QUIZ 37

1st Grade Spelling	The Rockies are M-O-U-N-T-A-I-N-S.
1st Grade Social Studies	19th century.
2nd Grade Animal Science	False. The raccoon is not a marsupial. It is a nocturnal mammal in the procyon genus.
2nd Grade Phys. Ed.	D. Individual medley.
3rd Grade Math	The place value is hundred thousand.
3rd Grade Earth Science	C. Those are examples of sedimentary rock.
4th Grade World Geography	A. The longest river in Europe is the Volga (2,290 miles long).
4th Grade World History	C. Royal tombs.
5th Grade English	C. Agony and ecstasy.
5th Grade Astronomy	The Gemini program put pairs of astronauts in orbit.
$1,000,000	The pop-up toaster was invented first, 1919. The lie detector was invented in 1921, frozen food and TV in 1923.

Quiz 38

1st Grade Dance	Tap dancing.
1st Grade Animal Science	False. Mammals always breathe through lungs.
2nd Grade Social Studies	C. Beavers like to build their own dams.
2nd Grade Animal Science	The cheetah is the fastest land animal. It can run up to 65 miles per hour.
3rd Grade Math	C. The corner of a square is a right angle.
3rd Grade World Geography	Cameroon is in Africa.
4th Grade Spelling	K-I-D-N-E-Y.
4th Grade U.S. History	Memphis, Tennessee.
5th Grade Physical Science	RADAR.
5th Grade Literature	H.G. Wells.
$1,000,000	P-T-E-R-O-D-A-C-T-Y-L.

Quiz 39

1st Grade English	C. The word "cannot" isn't a contraction.
1st Grade Phys. Ed.	Three.
2nd Grade Math	One-fifth of 15 is 3.
2nd Grade Math	42 dots.
3rd Grade Social Studies	C. It is called inflation when prices go up.
3rd Grade Animal Science	True.
4th Grade U.S. History	Lee Harvey Oswald is believed to have been JFK's assassin.
4th Grade Art	D. Cave walls.
5th Grade Spelling	I-R-R-I-G-A-T-I-O-N.
5th Grade Animal Science	C. Spine.
$1,000,000	Persia.

Quiz 40

1st Grade Science	D. Granite has no cells.
1st Grade Arithmetic	False. You would need 24 chairs to have six rows of four.
2nd Grade Vocabulary	D. Rain.
2nd Grade Animal Science	B. You're most apt to see a gator in Florida.

3rd Grade U.S. History	Franklin Delano Roosevelt was elected to four terms and served the longest (1933–45).
3rd Grade Biology	D. 4.
4th Grade U.S. Geography	Appalachian Mountains.
4th Grade Earth Science	The four cardinal directions are north, south, east and west.
5th Grade Social Studies	Ronald Reagan.
5th Grade World History	Sir Walter Raleigh.
$1,000,000	The Netherlands (Holland).

QUIZ 41

1st Grade U.S. Geography	Mexico is just south of Texas.
1st Grade Science	Mammalia, or Mammal.
2nd Grade Grammar	Three: brown, bleached and wet.
2nd Grade Health	Wheat is a grain.
3rd Grade Spelling	J-U-L-I-E-T.
3rd Grade Dance	Flamenco.
4th Grade Astronomy	The closest planet to the Sun is Mercury.
4th Grade Chemistry	Hydrogen.
5th Grade Music	B. The baritone sax can hit the lowest note.
5th Grade Animal Science	The shell is called the exoskeleton.
$1,000,000	We are in the Cenozoic era.

QUIZ 42

1st Grade Phys. Ed.	A. Baseball.
1st Grade Social Studies	July. Americans celebrate Independence Day on the 4th of July.
2nd Grade History	Columbus's ships were the *Niña*, the *Pinta*, and the *Santa Maria*.
2nd Grade World Geography	Mongolia is in Asia.
3rd Grade Animal Science	The slowest land mammal is the three-toed sloth.
3rd Grade Human Science	False. The hyoid bone is in your throat.
4th Grade U.S. Geography	Lake Ontario is the smallest of the Great Lakes.

4th Grade Measurements & Math	There are 3,600 seconds in an hour.
5th Grade U.S. History	True. Pigs were originally brought to North America from Europe.
5th Grade Math	The height of the triangle is 10 inches.
$1,000,000	C. Monet's paintings were examples of Impressionism.

Quiz 43

1st Grade Spelling	E-M-P-T-Y.
1st Grade Animal Science	D. Near the North Pole.
2nd Grade Animal Science	False. Crabs also live in rivers and lakes.
2nd Grade Spelling	B-A-S-K-E-T-B-A-L-L.
3rd Grade World Geography	Rome is the capital of Italy.
3rd Grade Health	C. Mumps.
4th Grade Math	A polygon must have more than two sides. A triangle is a polygon with the least possible number of sides.
4th Grade English	The American Revolution occurred while Rip Van Winkle was asleep.
5th Grade Math	10. The square root of 100 is 10.
5th Grade Social Studies	C. Farms.
$1,000,000	False—but it's endangered.

Quiz 44

1st Grade Literature	Whoville.
1st Grade U.S. Geography	The four U.S. states that border Mexico are Texas, New Mexico, Arizona and California.
2nd Grade World Geography	False. Mexico is in the northern hemisphere.
2nd Grade Spelling	A-R-C-T-I-C.
3rd Grade Astronomy	True.
3rd Grade Animal Science	C. Ocean.
4th Grade Math	The runway is 60,000 square yards in size.
4th Grade Phys. Ed.	D. Aerobics do not build big muscles.
5th Grade U.S. History	Stick.
5th Grade World History	Nero.
$1,000,000	B. 30 years.

1st Grade English	Jack Spratt could eat no fat.
1st Grade Animal Science	The polar bear is the largest type of bear.
2nd Grade Earth Science	True.
2nd Grade Social Studies	The Great Pyramid of Giza.
3rd Grade Math	There are 170 students in total.
3rd Grade U.S. Geography	Montana is farther west.
4th Grade Earth Science	It is called the Continental Divide, or sometimes the Great Divide.
4th Grade U.S. Geography	The capital of Tennessee is Nashville.
5th Grade Astronomy	C. At last count, scientists had discovered 63 moons orbiting Jupiter.
5th Grade Social Studies	D. Saudi Arabia.
$1,000,000	Sir Walter Scott wrote *Ivanhoe.*

QUIZ 46

1st Grade English	The word "too" should be spelled "two."
1st Grade Phys. Ed.	You could 1) hit your opponent with the ball, or 2) catch a ball in the air that was thrown by your opponent.
2nd Grade Animal Science	False. There are Komodo Dragons still living today.
2nd Grade Measurements	There are 4 pecks in a bushel.
3rd Grade U.S. History	Washington, D.C.
3rd Grade World Geography	D. Arctic.
4th Grade Social Studies	B. Japan.
4th Grade U.S. Geography	Yosemite National Park is in California.
5th Grade Art	C. Andy Warhol.
5th Grade Literature	Paris.
$1,000,000	$y = 12$. $5 \times 12 = 60$. $60 \div 3 = 20$.

QUIZ 47

1st Grade Spelling	BFF means Best F-R-I-E-N-D-S Forever.
1st Grade Phys. Ed.	You could 1) catch a kicked ball in the air, or 2) hit a runner with the ball when he or she is not on a base.
2nd Grade Astronomy	A. Venus.

2nd Grade Earth Science	True. Snowflakes are crystals.
3rd Grade Math	27.
3rd Grade Animal Science	An insect (the silkworm).
4th Grade Geography	The Chang River (3,964 miles), formerly known as the Yangtze, is the longest river in Asia.
4th Grade U.S. History	William Penn.
5th Grade Social Studies	Muhammad Ali.
5th Grade U.S. History	Lyndon Johnson.
$1,000,000	C. Bubble gum was invented first, in 1928. Scotch tape was invented in 1930, the electron microscope in 1931, and the jet engine in 1937.

Quiz 48

1st Grade Astronomy	9.
1st Grade Animal Science	D. A toad is an amphibian.
2nd Grade Phys. Ed.	C. 11.
2nd Grade Animal Science	The cheetah's natural habitat is Africa.
3rd Grade Math	There are 360 degrees in a circle.
3rd Grade Astronomy	C. 96 million.
4th Grade Literature	Robert Louis Stevenson.
4th Grade World Geography	India.
5th Grade Literature	Jonathan Swift.
5th Grade Earth Science	Sonar.
$1,000,000	The nose.

Quiz 49

1st Grade Grammar	Two. "Is" should be "are," and "sentence" is spelled with a c.
1st Grade Art	Sphinx.
2nd Grade Animal Science	True.
2nd Grade Astronomy	Sputnik, which went into orbit in 1957.
3rd Grade Social Studies	New Orleans, Louisiana.
3rd Grade Life Science	A. The lungs are part of the respiratory system.
4th Grade U.S. History	The Wright Brothers flew the first airplane in 1903.
4th Grade Math	It will take 4 hours and 30 minutes.

5th Grade Art	D. The Renaissance.
5th Grade Life Science	D. Neutrons.
$1,000,000	A. Southeast Asia, between Vietnam and Thailand.

QUIZ 50

1st Grade Animal Science	False. The T. rex was a meat-eater.
1st Grade English	3. Horse, barn, oats.
2nd Grade Measurements	Quart.
2nd Grade Geography	Antarctica.
3rd Grade Earth Science	San Francisco.
3rd Grade Social Studies	Of the U.S. states, Florida produces the most citrus fruit.
4th Grade U.S. Geography	The capital of Virginia is Richmond.
4th Grade History	Chicago.
5th Grade Social Studies	Administration.
5th Grade Astronomy	Chuck Yeager.
$1,000,000	Zorro fought bad guys in California when it was owned by Mexico.

QUIZ 51

1st Grade Literature	She is a spider.
1st Grade World Geography	The "Great Wall" is in China.
2nd Grade Earth Science	That ocean current is called the Gulf Stream because it originates in the Gulf of Mexico.
2nd Grade Phys. Ed.	C. Long jump.
3rd Grade U.S. Geography	The Grand Canyon is in Arizona.
3rd Grade Geometry	A 90-degree angle is a right angle.
4th Grade Astronomy	Jupiter.
4th Grade Chemistry	The letter K signifies potassium on the periodic table.
5th Grade U.S. History	C. The Civil War.
5th Grade Spelling	H-I-B-E-R-N-A-T-I-O-N.
$1,000,000	Johannes Gutenberg.

QUIZ 52

1st Grade English	The word "but" is the conjunction in that sentence.

1st Grade U.S. History	1969.
2nd Grade Earth Science	Sunlight.
2nd Grade World Geography	Bosnia is in Europe.
3rd Grade World History	The arena was known as the Colosseum.
3rd Grade Health	True. Your scapula is in your shoulder.
4th Grade U.S. Geography	Lake Michigan is the largest of the Great Lakes in surface area, beating Lake Superior 22,300 square miles to 20,600 square miles.
4th Grade Life Science	B. Follicle.
5th Grade Literature	The character's name is Stanley.
5th Grade Biology	The cerebrum is the part of your brain that allows you to think.
$1,000,000	William Henry Harrison. He caught pneumonia at his inauguration and died 31 days into his term.

QUIZ 53

1st Grade World History	Ferdinand and Isabella.
1st Grade World Geography	Ottawa is the capital of Canada.
2nd Grade U.S. History	Abraham Lincoln was born in Illinois.
2nd Grade Social Studies	Charles Lindbergh.
3rd Grade Math	117.
3rd Grade English	3. Brown, barking and red.
4th Grade Measurements	There are sixteen ounces in a pint.
4th Grade Literature	Beverly Cleary.
5th Grade Astronomy	Viking.
5th Grade Literature	B. Tennyson.
$1,000,000	South Africa.

QUIZ 54

1st Grade Art	Yellow, the color of the dandelions.
1st Grade U.S. Geography	C. Honolulu.
2nd Grade English	2. They are briskly and roughly.
2nd Grade World Geography	Indian Ocean.
3rd Grade Animal Science	False. Spiders are not insects.
3rd Grade World History	A. 1200s.
4th Grade Math	The 30 by 30 square has 900 square feet. The 5 by 200 rectangle has 1,000

square feet, so the rectangle has a greater area.

4th Grade U.S. History	The stock market crashed in 1929.
5th Grade Literature	B. The name of the character is Miss Honey.
5th Grade Computer	Google is known as a search engine.
$1,000,000	Resolution is measured in dots per inch.

Quiz 55

1st Grade Music	He gives the dog a bone.
1st Grade Science	C. An anemometer is used to measure wind speed.
2nd Grade Measurements	March, April and May have 92 days. September, October and November only have 91 days.
2nd Grade Earth Science	Humidity.
3rd Grade U.S. History	New Amsterdam.
3rd Grade Astronomy	Jupiter has the "eye," which is actually a huge hurricane-like storm that has been going on for millions of years.
4th Grade U.S. Geography	The capital of West Virginia is Charleston.
4th Grade U.S. History	Herbert Hoover was in the White House before FDR.
5th Grade Social Studies	Intelligence.
5th Grade Literature	Edgar Allan Poe.
$1,000,000	December.

Quiz 56

1st Grade English	"Apple" and "worm" are the two nouns in the sentence.
1st Grade History	Neil Armstrong was the first man on the Moon.
2nd Grade World Geography	True. The United States is in the Western Hemisphere.
2nd Grade Measurements	There are 80 pints in ten gallons (eight pints per gallon).
3rd Grade U.S. History	The War of 1812.

3rd Grade Earth Science	Moving water.
4th Grade Music	C. Italy.
4th Grade World History	A. Greece.
5th Grade Spelling	W-A-T-E-R-L-O-O.
5th Grade Math	27.
$1,000,000	Homer.

QUIZ 57

1st Grade U.S. History	He traveled around the U.S. planting apple trees.
1st Grade Spelling	J-U-R-A-S-S-I-C.
2nd Grade Animal Science	From the tusks of elephants.
2nd Grade Social Studies	Morse Code.
3rd Grade Earth Science	Mercury.
3rd Grade Astronomy	C. 250,000 miles.
4th Grade Geography	The longest river in South America is the Amazon (4,000 miles long).
4th Grade Computer	It's called spam.
5th Grade Social Studies & Spelling	I-N-V-E-S-T-I-G-A-T-I-O-N.
5th Grade Art	A mosaic.
$1,000,000	A. The computer came last, invented in 1946. The ballpoint pen was invented in 1938, the helicopter in 1939, and color TV in 1940.

QUIZ 58

1st Grade English	Children.
1st Grade Animal Science	D. A tadpole turning into a frog is called metamorphosis.
2nd Grade Earth Science	Acorn.
2nd Grade Health	C. Fruits.
3rd Grade Math	True. An equilateral triangle (all three sides the same length) is always equiangular (all three angles the same number of degrees).
3rd Grade Animal Science	Cocoon.
4th Grade Science	B. Evolution.
4th Grade U.S. Geography	The capital of Georgia is Atlanta.
5th Grade U.S. History	C. Jimmy Carter was in the Navy.

5th Grade Dance	A dance for two people.
$1,000,000	B. The black bear is the state animal of West Virginia.

1st Grade English	That symbol (:) is a colon.
1st Grade U.S. History	False, but he did make the first feature-length cartoon.
2nd Grade Health	Gingivitis is another word for gum disease.
2nd Grade Spelling	Immediately and grateful.
3rd Grade Science	The outermost layer of the Earth is called the crust.
3rd Grade Math	The lowest prime number is 2.
4th Grade U.S. History	B. The Lewis and Clark Expedition began in 1803.
4th Grade World Geography	Mediterranean.
5th Grade English	C. 19th century.
5th Grade Social Studies	The T stands for Treaty.
$1,000,000	C. Allegro means play it fast.

QUIZ 60

1st Grade Math	Sum.
1st Grade Science	D. Cyclone.
2nd Grade Health	Fluoride.
2nd Grade Geography	Mount Rushmore is in South Dakota.
3rd Grade Science	D. The center of the Earth is known as the core.
3rd Grade Earth Science	B. Oil.
4th Grade Literature	Herman Melville.
4th Grade U.S. History	C. 1869.
5th Grade World History	Benito Mussolini.
5th Grade Animal Science	The platypus.
$1,000,000	D. x = 2y.

QUIZ 61

1st Grade Geography	Paris is the capital of France.
1st Grade Art	There are 64 crayons in the deluxe Crayola box.

2nd Grade U.S. History	The president's name is Zachary Taylor.
2nd Grade Music	Five musicians play in a quintet.
3rd Grade Health	C. Low salt.
3rd Grade English	The symbol (;) is called a semi-colon.
4th Grade Astronomy	When the Earth passes between the Moon and the Sun, it is called a lunar eclipse.
4th Grade Chemistry	Helium.
5th Grade World Geography	Saudi Arabia.
5th Grade Social Studies	C. Mexico.
$1,000,000	Dr. Christian Barnard of South Africa in 1967.

Quiz 62

1st Grade Phys. Ed.	C. Figure skating.
1st Grade Literature	They cried.
2nd Grade Math	825 questions.
2nd Grade World Geography	Norway is in Europe.
3rd Grade Social Studies	The *Spirit of St. Louis*.
3rd Grade Human Science	False. Your coccyx is your tailbone, at the base of your spine.
4th Grade Grammar	C. "Quickly" is an adverb.
4th Grade U.S. Geography	Tallahassee is the capital of Florida.
5th Grade Literature	19th century.
5th Grade Phys. Ed.	26 miles.
$1,000,000	C. 30,000 years ago.

Quiz 63

1st Grade Animal Science	False. The chimpanzee is an ape.
1st Grade Music	Lyrics.
2nd Grade Astronomy	Lion.
2nd Grade U.S. History	Philadelphia.
3rd Grade Social Studies	C. Coal mining is an important industry in West Virginia.
3rd Grade Measurements	1,200 months.
4th Grade Math	The radius is 4 inches.
4th Grade Music	17th century.
5th Grade Human Science	B. 500 muscles.

| 5th Grade Music | Wolfgang. (His middle name was Amadeus.) |
| **$1,000,000** | The three main parts of an ant's body are the head (front), the thorax (middle), and the abdomen (rear). |

Quiz 64

1st Grade Health	D. Germs.
1st Grade U.S. Geography	The Alamo is in Texas.
2nd Grade Science	A. The Moon causes the tides.
2nd Grade U.S. History	A. The Chief Justice of the Supreme Court is the head of the judicial branch of the U.S. government.
3rd Grade Animal Science	Milk.
3rd Grade English	Airport is the compound word.
4th Grade Geometry	An octagon has eight sides.
4th Grade Grammar	B. Tall and short.
5th Grade Social Studies	C. 1920s.
5th Grade English	William Shakespeare in *Macbeth*.
$1,000,000	D. Pyotr Tchaikovsky wrote *The Nutcracker*.

Quiz 65

1st Grade Measurements	9 feet.
1st Grade History	Submarine.
2nd Grade Health	C. Shaking hands.
2nd Grade Vocabulary	Altitude.
3rd Grade Math	The 6 is the ten thousands digit.
3rd Grade Earth Science	Chlorophyll.
4th Grade Astronomy	Saturn is the second largest planet in the solar system.
4th Grade U.S. History	C. The most common first name for U.S. presidents is James.
5th Grade World History	Joseph Stalin.
5th Grade Math	$y = 36$.
$1,000,000	B. The euphonium is also known as the tenor tuba.

QUIZ 66

1st Grade English	The word "ran" is the verb in the sentence.
1st Grade Social Studies	President Ulysses S. Grant's likeness is on the fifty-dollar bill.
2nd Grade World Geography	False. China is in the Eastern Hemiphere.
2nd Grade Animal Science	False. Penguins live almost exclusively in the southern hemisphere. (The arctic region is near the North Pole.)
3rd Grade Math	There are 276 football players in total.
3rd Grade Spelling	H-O-R-I-Z-O-N-T-A-L.
4th Grade Measurements	There are 48 fluid ounces in three pints (16 ounces per pint).
4th Grade Geography	The tallest mountain in North America is Mount McKinley (20,320 feet).
5th Grade U.S. History	Harry Truman was president when World War II ended.
5th Grade Astronomy	Galaxies.
$1,000,000	B. $A = s \times s$.

QUIZ 67

1st Grade Spelling	I before E except after C.
1st Grade Geography	West.
2nd Grade Grammar	That symbol (&) is called an ampersand, or more commonly an "and sign."
2nd Grade Measurements	There are 16 ounces in a pound.
3rd Grade Social Studies	B. Cultured pearls were invented in Japan.
3rd Grade Music	A. The theremin is not a keyboard instrument. It is an electronic instrument often heard in old science fiction and horror movies.
4th Grade Math	The surface area of the cube is 150 square inches.
4th Grade Geography	Santa Fe is the capital of New Mexico.
5th Grade Math	D. Acute.

5th Grade U.S. History	B. Cuban Missile Crisis.
$1,000,000	Yucca Flat, Nevada.

1st Grade U.S. History	There are thirteen stripes on the U.S. flag, one for each of the original states.
1st Grade Animal Science	Fish breathe with gills.
2nd Grade Grammar	Two. "Geese" and "raindrops" are plural nouns.
2nd Grade Spelling	Q-U-I-E-T.
3rd Grade World Geography	False. It goes well north of Australia.
3rd Grade Human Science	The human heart is a muscle.
4th Grade U.S. Geography	The Great Lakes are Ontario, Erie, Michigan, Superior and Huron.
4th Grade U.S. Geography	Montgomery is the capital of Alabama.
5th Grade Chemistry	Carbon.
5th Grade Computer	It stands for World Wide Web.
$1,000,000	The world's largest fish is the whale shark, which averages thirty feet in length.

1st Grade Reading	Dr. Seuss.
1st Grade Art	Smock.
2nd Grade Animal Science	B. Reptile.
2nd Grade Social Studies	The U.N. is headquartered in New York City.
3rd Grade U.S. History	General George Armstrong Custer.
3rd Grade Science	B. The troposphere is the lowest layer of Earth's atmosphere.
4th Grade Math	Eight is the dividend.
4th Grade World Geography	Africa.
5th Grade Science	At sea level, water boils at 212 degrees Fahrenheit.
5th Grade World Geography	A. Mount Aconcagua (22.834 feet) is the tallest mountain in South America.
$1,000,000	The aorta is the largest artery in the human body.

1st Grade Art	B. Red is a primary color.
1st Grade Math	Five days. Three days to get there and two days to get back.
2nd Grade Measurements	A mile is longer.
2nd Grade History	True.
3rd Grade Astronomy	C. You would be heaviest on Jupiter. Because it is the largest of the planets, gravity there is strongest, causing everything to weigh more.
3rd Grade World Geography	Greenland is the largest island on Earth, if you don't count Australia.
4th Grade Math	Six. There are 9, 27, 45, 63, 81 and 99.
4th Grade English	Three (the, a, an).
5th Grade U.S. Geography	Maryland and Virginia both border the District of Columbia.
5th Grade World Geography	The second largest country in terms of area is Canada.
$1,000,000	$y = 2x$.

QUIZ 71

1st Grade History	D. Brazil.
1st Grade Measurements	Seven. January, March, May, July, August, October and December have 31 days.
2nd Grade Math	There are 72 hours in 3 days.
2nd Grade Animal Science	The giant panda's natural habitat is in Asia.
3rd Grade Math	None. A scalene triangle always has corners with three different angles.
3rd Grade Geography	The Tropic of Cancer is in the northern hemisphere.
4th Grade Astronomy	The five planets that can be seen with the naked eye are Mercury, Venus, Mars, Jupiter and Saturn.
4th Grade Chemistry	Krypton, the element—not Superman's original planet.
5th Grade U.S. History	The U.S. Constitution was written in 1787.

| 5th Grade Social Studies | The official currency of Puerto Rico is the U.S. dollar. |
| **$1,000,000** | 1.0. |

1st Grade Geography	Australia is both a country and a continent.
1st Grade Art	Red and yellow, when mixed together, make orange.
2nd Grade Social Studies	South America.
2nd Grade Life Science	True. A hummingbird can fly backward.
3rd Grade Math	Each girl gets 414 gumballs.
3rd Grade Human Science	True. The lower back is known as the lumbar region.
4th Grade Measurements	366. Since 1980 was a leap year, February had an extra day.
4th Grade Social Studies	A potential candidate must have been a resident of the U.S. for 14 years to run for president.
5th Grade World Geography	Corsica is part of France.
5th Grade Physical Science	Density describes the mass of an object divided by *volume*.
$1,000,000	C. Anthropomorphism.

QUIZ 73

1st Grade Animal Science	False. (It's a mammal.)
1st Grade Social Studies	Andrew Jackson's image appears on the $20 bill.
2nd Grade Animal Science	True. The opossum is a marsupial.
2nd Grade Art	Red and blue when mixed together make purple.
3rd Grade Geology	True.
3rd Grade History	There are 100 decades in a millennium.
4th Grade Math	Ten. 5, 15, 25, 35, 45, 55, 65, 75, 85 and 95.
4th Grade Geometry	B. One.
5th Grade Music	D. A clarinet is a reed instrument.

5th Grade Social Studies	C. Tecumseh was the name of the chief of the Shawnee Indians. He was killed in battle with U.S. troops in 1813.
$1,000,000	Talc.

Quiz 74

1st Grade Arithmetic	$1 + 2 + 3 + 4 + 5 + 6 + 7 + 8 + 9 = 45$.
1st Grade Geography	Alabama.
2nd Grade Social Studies	Spanish.
2nd Grade Astronomy	Two. Mars has two moons, Phobos and Deimos.
3rd Grade Geometry	A polygon must have at least three corners.
3rd Grade Math	B. Henry ate half the pie.
4th Grade Art	Vincent van Gogh painted that masterpiece—after actually cutting off a piece of his own ear.
4th Grade English	The word "briskly" is the adverb, as it describes the verb "walked."
5th Grade World History	Zeus.
5th Grade Social Studies	A. The Canadian Shield is a plateau in eastern Canada that stretches from the Arctic Ocean in the north to the Great Lakes in the south.
$1,000,000	B. 70.

Quiz 75

1st Grade Arithmetic	The difference is 47. $111 - 64 = 47$.
1st Grade Grammar	The word "him" is the pronoun.
2nd Grade English	The plural of moose is moose.
2nd Grade Science	Using the Fahrenheit scale, water freezes at 32 degrees.
3rd Grade Earth Science	C. Entomologists study insects.
3rd Grade U.S. Geography	B. Lincoln.
4th Grade Math	A. 8.
4th Grade U.S. History	C. John Wilkes Booth.
5th Grade Math	B. .45.

5th Grade Social Studies

$1,000,000

C. Spain had a permanent settlement in St. Augustine, Florida, by 1565.
The occipital lobe controls sight. It is located at the top back of the head.

About the Author

MICHAEL BENSON is the author of more than fifty books and the proud father of a 5th grader. He is a recognized expert in pop culture, and has published works about film, sports, and national defense. He is the author of Complete Idiot's Guides to professional wrestling, modern China, aircraft carriers, submarines, motorcycle choppers, the CIA, and national security. He has written biographies of Ronald Reagan, Bill Clinton, William Howard Taft, Dale Earnhardt, Jeff Gordon, Gloria Estefan, Hank Aaron, Wayne Gretzky, and Muhammad Ali. He is the former editor of *Fight Game*, *All Time Baseball Greats*, and *Military Technical Journal* magazines. Originally from Rochester, New York, Benson is a graduate of Hofstra University and currently lives in Brooklyn with his wife and two children.